the book,
spiritual instrument

For Lucas
with much love
Christmas, 1996

mom & Larry

the book
spiritual
instrument

edited by

JEROME ROTHENBERG

and

DAVID GUSS

Granary Books
New York City 1996

The publisher wi[...]
contributors [...]
reprint th[...]
and [...]
C[...]

...shes to thank the
...or permission to
...eir work. Acknowledgement
...hanks are also extended to
...harlie Morrow and The New
Wilderness Foundation who first
published *The Book, Spiritual
Instrument* as *New Wilderness Letter* #11
in 1982. Gershom Scholem's
selection is from *On the Kabbalah
and its Symbolism.* Copyright © 1965
by Schocken Books Inc. Reprinted
by permission of Schocken Books,
published by Pantheon Books,
a division of Random House, Inc.

Printed and bound in The United
States of America

ISBN 1-887123-08-3

Library of Congress # 96-77362

First Granary Books Edition 1996

Book design by Diane Bertolo

Cover photograph by Michael Gibbs

Steven Clay
Granary Books, Inc.
568 Broadway, Suite 403
New York, NY 10012, U S A

Tel: (212) 226-5462
Fax: (212) 226-6143
E-mail: sclay@interport.net
Web site: www.granarybooks.com

Available to the trade through:
D.A.P./Distributed Art Publishers
636 Broadway, 12th Floor,
New York, NY 10012, USA

Tel: (212) 473-5119
Fax: (212) 673-2887

Contents

Pre-face (1996)

"Thought is made in the mouth," said Tristan Tzara,
and Edmond Jabès: "The book is as old as fire and water"
—and both, we know, were right.

WHEN I WROTE THAT in 1977, I was coming out of a shared engagement with the history & present possibility of song & speech as the basis for a new poetics of performance. But I was also involved (in thought & in practice) with the still living presence of the book & writing—an involvement that I clearly felt some urgency to voice. Along with that was a need to understand both vocal & visual language in all their manifestations & extensions, & it was this need, this desire, say, that formed the basis for what I & others had recently been speaking of as *ethnopoetics*. Still more there was a recognition that any exploration of language that took us into what I came to think of as areas of deep culture (wherever found) was at the same time a descent into the domain of deep mind, or, if I can say so without blurring the issue, into the domain of *spirit* as such.

It was considerations of this kind that led me to work with David Guss on the assemblage that follows. In doing so there were two widely separated guides who brought the connections together in my mind: the Mexican (Mazatec) shamaness María Sabina & the pivotal French symbolist poet Stéphane Mallarmé. Unlettered & speaking only Mazatec, Sabina conceived the key to Language & to her own Language-centered chanting in the form of a great Book of Language or as "little luminous objects that fall from heaven" to be caught "word after word with my hands." Both of her images rhymed for me with others that had come to us principally from Mallarmé—the latter as if it prefigured the typographical castings & recastings of his master poem, *Un coup de dès*; the former his vision of the book as "spiritual instrument… the [single] Book that every writer worked at even without knowing…the Orphic explanation of the Earth, which is the poet's only duty."

What Guss & I set out to do, then, was to assemble a number of such rhymings: historical & contemporary instances from cultures (both literate & oral) that offered alternative visions of the book, set side by side with Mallarméan & post-Mallarméan experiments with what Karl Young, as a latterday practitioner, speaks of below as "bookforms." The beginnings of such a comparative—& ethnopoetic—project went back to *Alcheringa*, the journal of ethnopoetics that Dennis Tedlock & I had co-founded in the early 1970s. With an eye toward deeply rooted works & practices that could (re)illuminate our present workings, we left room for instances of traditional or early written art: paleolithic calendar notations, Egyptian & Mayan hieroglyphs, recastings of Bible & other Jewish bookworks, Old Norse runes, & Navajo pictographs (to name a few that come immediately to mind). It seemed clear—as *Alcheringa* moved into its final breakup—that this was an area in need of further exploration. For that I struck out on my own in *A Big Jewish Book* (later revised as *Exiled in the Word*), where I could focus on the written alongside—& drawing from—the oral, & with a strong awareness of how central the book was in that highly charged, sometimes over-determined context. And I found the same play—between oral & written torahs—entering not only my own work but that of other contemporaries & friends: Meltzer, Hirschman, Duncan, Schwerner, even one, say, like Jabès, so centered on "the book" that we forget the almost equal value that his work gives to "the voice."

In the years immediately before & after I separated from *Alcheringa*, I had assisted Charlie Morrow in the formation of the New Wilderness Foundation, which sought—not only in music, which was Morrow's mainstay, but across the spectrum of the arts—to explore the relation between old & new forms of art-making. As an offshoot of the foundation & a follow-up as well to *Alcheringa*, Morrow backed me in launching a successor magazine, *New*

Wilderness Letter, to offer occasional but pointed coverage of matters that concerned us then: the poetry & art of numbers, of dreams, of signs & signing in the language of the deaf, & so on. I set out our intentions as follows in the opening "statement":

> ...The editor—a poet by inclination & practice—recognizes *poesis* in all arts & sciences, all human thoughts & acts directed toward such ends: the participation in what the surrealist master André Breton called a "sacred action" or what Gary Snyder defined as the "real work of modern man: to uncover the inner structure & actual boundaries of the mind." The *New Wilderness Letter* will therefore not be specialized & limited by culture or profession but will be a report, largely through the creative work itself, of where that process takes us.

With that as opener, an advisory board of sorts—more avant-garde & art-centered than that of *Alcheringa*—started slowly to form, consisting (by the end of the venture) of David Antin, Eleanor Antin, Helen Mayer Harrison, Newton Harrison, Dick Higgins, Allan Kaprow, Jackson Mac Low, Steve McCaffery, Linda Montano, Charlie Morrow, & Pauline Oliveros. From the seventh issue on I was joined by Barbara Einzig as associate editor, & from the tenth by Einzig & David Guss together.

The eleventh issue of *New Wilderness Letter* (1982)—& the last one in its original format—consisted of the work presented in the present publication & subtitled, after Mallarmé, *The Book, Spiritual Instrument*. It was our intention here to show "the book" on a level with those other forms of language & language-art that Guss & I, as independent assemblers, had earlier engaged in bringing forward. Guss's work as translator & editor had spanned a range from *The Selected Poetry of Vicente Huidobro* to translations (& later to field studies) of the lore & rituals of the Makiritare people of Venezuela, & the breadth of his understandings was exemplified in *The Language of the Birds*, a gathering of works—ancient & modern, mythic & historic—that touch on the intercommunication of human beings & other animal species. By 1982 he was studying folklore and anthropology at UCLA, while I was living down in San Diego & teaching between campuses there & elsewhere in southern California. The desire to bridge the gap between poetics & ethnopoetics and to extend our discourse to the full range of visible languages was by now intense.

The opening wedge came from Michael Gibbs's translation & visual commentary on Mallarmé's *Le livre, instrument spirituel,* which not only brought us back to the first modernist breakthroughs but also provided a context in which those breakthroughs corresponded to an ancient sense of book as sacred object. We were visited at the same time by Eduardo Calderón Palomino, a remarkable artist & traditional *curandero* from Peru, who not only was a book reader in the usual sense but (at David Guss's suggestion) had also given a full & articulate discussion of his *mesa* (healing altar) as an assemblage of objects that could be read the way one reads a book. In our minds, then, Calderón rhymed with Mallarmé in much the way that María Sabina did, & that rhyming suggested a series of links, a web of ancient & modern possibilities that could be woven into a new display or book. And, since I had previously published excerpts from María Sabina's chants alongside Henry Munn's germinal essay, "Writing in the Imagination of an Oral Poet" (*New Wilderness Letter* 5/6), we didn't return to her but looked for other examples to bring into our mix.

Those other examples—many gathered in earlier explorations—fell quickly into place. On the ethnopoetic side, J. Stephen Lansing's essay showed the intricate connection between written text & its necessary sounding in traditional Balinese performance; Dennis Tedlock drew from his translation (then in progress) of the Mayan *Popol Vuh* a series of comments on the nature of the book & writing; Tina Oldknow offered (as "Muslim Soup") an account of the efficacy of written (sacred) words when the material used in the writing is removed & decocted in an herbal mixture; & Karl Young provided a speculative analysis of the Mixtec *Codex Vienna,* one of the surviving illuminated books from ancient Mexico. At the same time Young appeared again with an illustrated set of his own sculptural "bookforms," reflective of a widespread contemporary concern with the physical & graphic dimension of books & with the text as printed surface. A similar concern with "bookforms" (writ large) was Alison Knowles's monumental *The Book of Bean,* a walk-through work enhanced in the presentation by her own remarks & George Quasha's accompanying "auto-dialogue [reflections] on the transvironmental book." Additional writings & commentaries came from Fluxus artist/poet Dick Higgins; from Jed Rasula in a string of definitions & pata(pseudo)definitions of Greek derivatives associated with the text & speaking; from Edmond Jabès, whose interview displays a typically Jabèsean connection between the hypostatized book & the desert (= wilderness in other contexts); from David Meltzer, like Jabès (but independently) the creator of imagined rabbis & their imagined dream books; from Gershom Scholem, a setting forth of the interpenetration in mystical Judaism of "oral tradition and the written word"; & from Herbert Blau, a supplement to Lansing's "sounding of the text" & a wide-ranging yet personal discussion of his own & others' practice in a theater of (always) heightened means. Finally, Becky Cohen provided a series of striking photo portraits in which a number of contemporary American poets are shown in the act of reading, making of the book (as it were) "an instrument of performance."

In saying all of this there is no attempt of course to claim completeness then or now. Rather, as the editors of a magazine addressed to a particular time & place, we hoped to suggest a number of instances of how the idea of book could be considered & reconsidered. The work, we thought, would be successful if it led to still further considerations & connections—even more so if it encouraged new works &, at a time of (merely) technological &/or mechanical breakthroughs, reminded us that the spiritual-in-art, but more pointedly its connection to *deep mind* & *deep culture*, might still be our concern. The approach in these pages is to that degree ideological, so that our attempt, say, to maintain an interface between the book & its performance is to be read against the history of those (supposedly) unalterable Books—the Bible foremost—that served, when used as such, to enslave rather than liberate the mind. It is in the amassing of alternatives—both old & new—that we may find our surest antidote to what that still portends.

J.R.
Encinitas, California
May 1996

Editor's Note (1982)

WHEN THE PRESENT SENIOR EDITOR left *Alcheringa* ("a first magazine of the world's tribal poetries") in 1976, it was with a sense that *New Wilderness Letter* wouldn't have to duplicate the ethnopoetic work contained therein but would concentrate on intersections between all arts & on those more recent explorations of mind, language, nature & society subsumed under the term "new wilderness." With the announced demise of *Alcheringa* there is, for me, an inevitable pull toward filling the gap it leaves & renewing the ethnopoetic project in this new & larger context. Toward that end, David Guss has joined me as an extraordinary co-worker—a poet himself & the editor/translator of poetries that range from the "creationism" of Vicente Huidobro to the Makiritare Indians' traditional Watunna cycle. Barbara Einzig continues in association as well, her recent dream-work issue of *New Wilderness Letter* another instance of the merging of ethnopoetic & experimental interests. And my own work has now come, full cycle, to the making of a revised *Technicians of the Sacred*—the book that was, for me, the turning point.

In *New Wilderness Letter* #11, the investigation turns again to the idea of book & writing, both as a persistent contemporary concern & as an often unacknowledged kingpin of a revitalized & expanded *ethno*poetics. If the foregrounding of oral tradition has seemed necessary in the face of the ongoing tyranny of literature & of "text" (in the more academicized lingo), it is time as well to assert that writing—as book and as performance—is not the exclusive gift of *this* as opposed to *that* "level" of culture. In an age of cybernetic breakthroughs, the experimental tradition of twentieth-century poetry & art has expanded our sense of language in all its forms, including the written. While doing this, it should also have sensitized us to the existence of a range of written traditions in those cultures we have named "non"- or "pre"-literate—extending the meaning of literacy beyond a system of (phonetic) letters to the practice of writing itself. But to grasp the actual possibilities of writing (as with any other form of language or of culture), it is necessary to know it in all its manifestations—new & old. It is our growing belief (more apparent now than at the start of the ethnopoetics project) that the cultural dichotomies between writing & speech—the "written" & the "oral"—disappear the closer we get to the source. To say again what seems so hard to get across: there is a primal book as there is a primal voice, & it is the task of our poetry & art to recover it—in our minds & in the world at large. [J.R.]

"THE BOOK WE WRITE CONTINUES TO BE WRITTEN"

. . . .

beautiful men &
beautiful women
come alive

we are at the beginning of
a dream
someone will have to write

the great book of the century
assembled
as dream-work

the authors move like children
into death
dancing like children

—Jerome Rothenberg

Le Livre, Instrument Spirituel
The Book,
Spiritual Instrument*

translated and visually interpreted by Michael Gibbs

A PROPOSITION which emanates from myself—whether cited variously as my eulogy or as blame—I claim it as my own together with all those that crowd in here—affirms, in short, that everything in the world exists in order to end up as a book.

The qualities required for this work, certainly genius, make me afraid, as one among the destitute—but not to halt there, and granted that the volume requires nobody to sign it, what is it?—the hymn, harmony and joy, grouped as a pure unity in some lightning circumstance, of the relations between everything. Man is entrusted with seeing divinely, because the bond, at will and pellucid, has to his eyes no other expression than in the parallelism of the sheet.

On a garden bench such a new publication lies; *I rejoice if the passing wind half opens and unintentionally animates aspects of the book's exterior*—several of which, because of the flood of things perceived, maybe nobody has thought of since reading existed. The opportunity to do it is when, liberated, the newspaper dominates, even my own, which I put aside, and it takes flight near the roses, anxious to smother their fervent and proud assembly—*spread out amidst the clump, I shall abandon it, and the flowering words, to their silence*, and, in a technical way, propose to note how such a tattered sheet differs from the book, itself pre-eminent. A newspaper remains the point of departure; literature discharges itself at will.

Thus—

With regard to the large printed sheet, the folding is a sign, almost religious, which is not so striking as its settling, in density, presenting *the minia-*

ture tomb, indeed, of the soul.

Everything that printing discovered is summarized under the name of the Press, up until now, in an elementary form in the newspaper—the sheet in itself, having received the imprint, exhibits, to the highest degree, crudely, the casting of a text. This usage, proximate or previous to the finished product, certainly has conveniences for the writer: posters joined end to end, proofs, which restore improvisation. So, in the same way, strictly speaking, with a 'daily' before there appears to the vision, little by little, but whose vision?, a meaning in the arrangement, a charm even, I would say, like a popular fairyland. Proceed—the elite or high-class of Paris, detached, superior, despite a thousand obstacles, attains disinterestedness and, following on from the situation, precipitates and stems, far away, as though by means of

an electric fire, after the articles that have appeared as a result of it, the original servitude: the announcement, on the fourth page, between an incoherence of inarticulate cries. A spectacle, moral even—what lacks the newspaper, with all its exploits, in order to wipe out the book—although, visibly yet, they are united simply, or rather basically, by the signatures, and the demand for generality of columns—(it lacks) nothing, or almost—as long as the book, such as it is, delays, like a weir, unconcerned, where the other empties itself... even the format, useless—and in vain does this extraordinary, gathered in like *a wing about to unfold,* intervention of the folding or the rhythm concur, initial cause for a closed sheet to contain a secret, where dwells the silence, precious, in pursuit of evocative signs, quite literally abolished for the spirit.

So, without the furling of the paper and the undersides that it establishes, *the shadow scattered in black characters* would not present a reason for spreading itself out, *like a wreckage of mystery,* on the surface, in the separation lifted up by the finger.

Newspaper, the spread sheet, assumes an untimely outcome from the impression, through simple maculation—there is no doubt that the vulgar, glaring advantage lies, in the eyes of everyone, in the multiplication of each copy, and the circulation. This benefaction bestows a miracle, in the higher sense, wherein the words, originally, are reduced to the usage, *capable of infinity almost to the point of sanctifying a language,* of some twenty letters— their growing, everything returning there so as to well up in a moment, the beginning—bringing the typographical composition close to a rite.

The book, total expansion of the letter, has to extract from it, directly, a

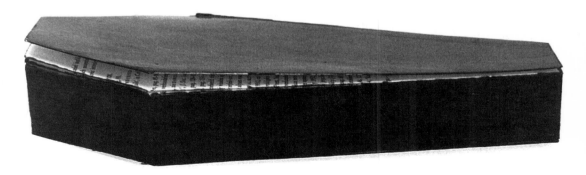

mobility and, being spacious, through connections, has to institute a game, we know not what, that confirms the fiction.

There is nothing fortuitous, there, where a chance seems to catch the idea, the apparatus is all the same—consequently do not judge these remarks, either in an industrial sense or in relation to materiality. The fabrication of the book, in the ensemble that will expand, begins with a phrase. Since time immemorial the poet knows the place of this verse, in the sonnet which is inscribed spiritually or onto pure space. As for myself, I disregard the volume and a marvel proclaimed by its structure if I cannot, knowingly, imagine such a motif with the idea of a *special place, the page and the height,* in its own everyday aspect or in terms of the work itself. Plus *the incessant coming and going* of looking, one line finishing and beginning again at the next one— such a practice does not represent the pleasure, having everlastingly broken with everything for one hour, of translating its chimera. Otherwise or unless it is executed actively, like pieces for piano, measured by the sheets, how could anyone not close his eyes to dream? Neither this presumption nor a

fastidious servility, but the initiative of whoever receives its lightning bolt, connects the fragmented notation.

Through reading, a solitary tacit concert presents itself to the spirit that regains, at a lower volume, the meaning —no mental means will be lacking to extol the symphony, rarefied, and that's everything—the act of thinking. Poetry, next to the idea, is Music, par excellence—it does not consent to inferiority.

Here in real life, nevertheless, as far as I am concerned, as regards pamphlets to be read in the current fashion, I brandish a knife, like the cook about to slit the fowl's neck.

The unopened virginal book, moreover, ready for a sacrifice from which the red edges of ancient books bleed; the introduction of a weapon, or page cutter, to establish the taking of possession. How personal the conscience previously, with this barbarous sham—when it would become participation, with the book purchased from here or from there, varied in likeness, divined like an enigma—almost remade by itself. The folds will perpetuate a mark, intact, inviting the sheet to be opened or closed, as the owner wishes. So blind and petty a process, this assault which is committed, through the destruction of a fragile inviolability. Our sympathy might go to the newspaper which is not exposed to this treatment—its influence, nonetheless, is disagreeable, imposing a monotony onto the complex organism, which literature requires, and onto the divine tome—always *the unbearable column* which is merely distributed there, page-sized, hundreds of times.

But …

—I hear, can there be any end to this; and in a moment I am going to satisfy the curiosity in every detail, for the work, preferably on its own, should provide an example. Why—a burst of grandeur, of thought or of emotion, eminent, a sentence pursued in large letters, one line per page, in a graduated arrangement—wouldn't this keep the reader in suspense throughout the whole book, appealing to this power of enthusiasm—all around, minor clusters, of secondary importance, explicatory or derivative—*an array of flourishes.*

The fashion of catching the sauntering reader unawares, through remote statement; I would agree, if many, whom I am friends with, do not notice, with the instinct coming from somewhere else which made them assemble their writings in an obsolete way, decoratively, between the sentence and the line of verse, certain characteristics similar to this; thus, if it is to be isolated, let it be so, for the sake of the renown of clairvoyance that the epoch clamours for, where everything is apparent. One divulges his intuition, theoretically and, it may well be, into the void, like time—he knows that such suggestions, which attain to the art of literature, have to commit themselves firmly. The hesitation, however, in discovering all of a sudden everything that does not yet exist, prudishly, to everyone's surprise, weaves a veil.

Let us attribute to our dreams, before reading, in a garden, the attention demanded by some white butterfly, this one that is *everywhere at once, nowhere,* it vanishes; but not before an acute and ingenious trifle, to which I reduce the subject, had, a moment ago, passed and repassed, insistently, before my astonished eyes.

J . STEPHEN LANSING

The Aesthetics of the Sounding of the Text

The word moves a bit of air and this the next until it reaches
the ear of one who hears it and is therein awakened.

NACHMAN OF BRATZLAV

Homage to the god...who is the essence of written letters...
concealed in the dust of the poet's pencil.

THE SUMANASANTAKA

THE OPPOSITIONS BETWEEN language and culture, speech and writing, langue and parole, are the foundations of modern semiotics, the fruits of what Foucault has described as the "discovery of language" in the last two centuries in the West. They define the parameters of our discourse on language, a discourse based on our developing cultural awareness of language as more than a colorless medium of expression. Thus, for example, Paul Ricoeur investigates the nature of language by asking, "What is a text?"—a question which leads him to the oppositions between speaking and writing, and language and the world. For Ricoeur, the defining quality of a written text is precisely that it exists outside the world: "a text is somehow 'in the air,' outside of the world or without a world; by means of this obliteration of all relation to the world, every text is free to enter in relation with all the other texts which come to take the place of the circumstantial reality shown by living speech." (D. Rasmussen, 1971:138) Speech, in other words, is physically present in the world—it occurs as an event in space and time—while texts hang in an unworldly suspension, awaiting a reader who may draw them into relationship with one another through the act of reading. Texts are in this sense timeless and detached from the world. Edward Said criticizes this view but regards it nonetheless as pervading, indeed defining our modern approach to texts. [1] In a recent interview, Said wonders that "our interpretive worldly-wisdom has been applied, in a sense, to everything except ourselves; we are brilliant at deconstructing the mystifications of a text, at elucidating the blindness of the critical methods, but we have seemed unable to apply these techniques to the very life of the texts in the world ..." The subject of this essay is the "life of the texts in the world," a topic which, as Said observes, appears only on the distant horizons of the Western critical traditions, but is central for the literate cultures of Southeast Asia. However, the purpose of this essay is not merely to show that others contrive to see the operations of speech and writing differently than we do. We aspire, after all, to a general theory of semiotics, a theory rich enough to accommodate the complex and interpenetrating relationships between language and culture, but our studies have so far been restricted to a very narrow range: the role of texts in Western cultures in the recent past. But the texts are not always novels or advertisements; there is more to Language than French and English— ours, in short, is not necessarily a privileged position. Therefore, the distinctions between speech and writing, and language and the world, which seem to us to be a starting point for analysis, are not necessarily obligatory.

The concept of the "sounding of the text" is drawn from the aesthetic vocabulary of several Southeast Asian cultures—in particular, the Balinese, whose libraries house texts in five languages, several of which are also commonly used in speech. This linguistic complexity, coupled with the brilliant theatrical traditions of the Balinese, makes Bali a particularly interesting case for studying the relationship of language to culture. But my purpose in this essay is not so much to explore the meaning of language in different cultures, but rather to attempt to introduce the notion of the sounding of the text as a semiotic principle.

1. For Said's critique of Ricouer, see Edward Said, "The Text, the World, the Critic," in Harari, 1979: 164-166.

The Power of the Sounded Word

In the Thai language, the word for text is *bot*. To interpret a text in a reading or performance is to *ti bot*: to "strike" the text, in the same sense that one "strikes" a musical gong to emit a note. Mattani Rutnin writes of Thai dancers interpreting a bot: "Those who can interpret the bot successfully, i.e., in terms of aesthetics, drama and emotion, are said to *ti bot tack* (literally, smash the text to pieces—interpret the text with utmost refinement and depth)" (1980). Thai aesthetics is therefore divisible into two branches:

      1. the aesthetics of the text/instrument,

      2. the aesthetics of the sounding of the text.

The first is analogous to modern Western aesthetics in that it involves a kind of iconographic analysis, concerned with questions of form, style and composition. But the aesthetics of the *sounding* of the text is directed to the question of the ways a text becomes manifest in a reading or performance. In the Thai view, these are quite different, if complementary branches of aesthetics. We might summarize the differences thus: one set of questions is raised if we talk about a sonnet in terms of its intrinsic qualities, as though existing perpetually in some timeless Platonic realm of art. But very different questions suggest themselves if we consider the sonnet as it is performed, as an event occurring within a culture. There is a pervasive tradition in Southeast Asia which insists that the sounding of words or music has intrinsic power. This power is beautifully evoked in Shelly Errington's analysis of the role of prose stories (*hikayat*) in Malay culture:

> Hikayat were written, but they were written to be read aloud in a public place. As such, they are better considered notes for a performance than texts to be read in quiet solitude. People listened to, rather than read, hikayat. They were attracted into its realm through the voice of the narrator, which carried (*membawa*) and brought into being the hikayat.
>
> Not uncommonly, the reading of the hikayat is one of the events related in hikayat. Sejarah Melayu, for instance, tells of a hikayat being read when the Portuguese attacked Malaka. One particularly sinister passage in *Hikayat Hang Tuah* tells that Hang Jebat is asked by the raja to recite hikayat. His sweet, clear, melo-

dious voice melts the hearts of listeners and renders them inexpressibly tender; the raja falls asleep on Hang Jebat's lap; and the palace women are inspired by lust and throw him betel nuts and perfume from behind the screen. The scene— or should we call it sound?—marks the beginning of Hang Jebat's treason. We hear of the power of words not only when hikayat are read. Words flow from Hang Tuah's mouth sweet as honey when he visits distant lands, and those around him feel love. The almost palpable physical imagery of the words flowing from his mouth points to their active presence in the world: they do not stand apart from the world, explaining it or representing it. They are a presence, having their effect in the world. Throughout the hikayat, the imagery of sounds and silence is pervasive. To *berdiam* is both to remain silent and do nothing. Of some-one who is helpless the hikayat says, *tidak kata-kata lagi* ("he spoke no more"). Hang Tuah himself is wounded by the Portuguese near the end of the hikayat and falls overboard, to be retrieved quickly by his compatriots. The hikayat does not describe his wounds or the blood. Its significance falls upon us, rather, as we hear that for three days and three nights he cannot speak. [1979:237]

The concept of the sounding of the text is based upon belief in the power of what Errington calls "formed sounds, whether of words in spells, or the read-ing of the sacred texts, or of gamelan music, or of the combination of music, voices and sounds in *wayang* (shadow play)." This belief in the power of "formed sounds" is widespread among Southeast Asian peoples, and appears to be very ancient. Certainly it has an archaic flavor, suggesting a rather naive or even "primitive" belief in word-magic.

But the impression of naivete is shattered as soon as we confront even the earliest written texts. Consider, for example, the literature now known as "Old Javanese," which came into being in the Hindu/Buddhist courts of Java beginning around the ninth century A.D. The first texts were poems, written in the tradition of Sanskrit literature, in a language which drew upon both Sanskrit and Javanese styles and vocabularies. Each poem begins with a *manggala*: an invocation, which sets forth the poet's understanding of the relationship between himself, his text and the world. The manggala begins by invoking one of the many gods and goddesses, but it is not so much the identity of the god invoked as the manner of the invocation and the aspect in which the deity is viewed that matters. And these appear to be the same despite the variety of names. The god concerned is always the god who is present in everything that can be described as *langö*, the god of beauty in the widest sense. He is found in the beauty of the mountains and sea, in the pleasure-garden with its charms of trees and flowers and in the month when they are in full bloom, in feminine grace and charm. It goes without saying that he resides in the lover's complaint and in the description of nature, in the feeling that beauty arouses in the heart of the lover and of the poet. He resides in everything used for giving expression to that feeling, whether it is the spoken or written word, and therefore also in sounds and letters and even in the instruments of writing. He is the god of the board that is written on and the pencil that is written with, and of the dust that is sent whirling about, finally to settle, by sharpening the latter. [Zoetmulder 1974:175]

The Sumanasantaka, for example, begins by invoking the god of "beauty" (*langö*) who is concealed in the dust of the pencil sharpened by the poet, and is asked to descend into the letters of the poem as if they were his temple. This god is considered to be both immanent and transcendent; immaterial (*niskala*); of a finer and subtler nature than the world, which is an object of the senses (*suksma*). It is through the apprehension of this "god," that one can pierce the veil of illusion (*maya*) to discover the nature of reality. This "god," then, is both the ultimate foundation of all that exists and also its real essence—imperceptible because it is of a finer texture than the perceptible world, but nonetheless pervading everything "from the coarse to the fine" (*aganal alit*).

Obviously, the English words "god" and "beauty" are imperfect translations for the concept of such a being, or essence, or experience. After a brave attempt at translation, Zoetmulder (the foremost student of Old Javanese) throws up his hands with the remark that translators "must resign themselves to the fact that Old Javanese is exceptionally rich in this area of description, and has developed a variety of means of expressing (aesthetic emotion)

A dancer performing a *baris* (warrior's dance), a type of *wali* (performance for the divine audience) at the temple Pura Ulun Danu Batur in central Bali.

which other languages simply do not possess." But Zoetmulder's remarks on the word *alangö* (which I have been rendering in the form "langö" as both "beauty" and "aesthetic experience") are helpful:

> Alangö means both "enraptured" and "enrapturing." It can be said of a beautiful view as well as of the person affected by its beauty. It has what we might call a "subjective" and an "objective" aspect, for there is a common element—the Indians would say: a common *rasa*—in both subject and object, which makes them connatural and fit to become one. Objectively langö is the quality by which an object appeals to the aesthetic sense. [Ibid:173]

Thus in one passage of the Sumanasantaka, the waves of the sea are described as a "flight of crystal stairs down which the poet descends when, in old age, he ends his life by plunging into langö." The same theme, of the way langö knits the essence of man and nature together, harmonizing the "Small" and "Great Worlds" (micro/macrocosm), is expressed in these lines from the poem quoted earlier, the Sumanasantaka:

When a woman wishes to die, she asks the gods to return her beauty to the month of Kartika, the loveliness of her hair to the rain-bearing clouds, the suppleness of her arms to the *welas-arep* creeper, her tears to the dew-drops suspended from the tip of a blade of grass. [Ibid: 209-210]

From Letters to Sounds

The concept of langö defines an aesthetics, and with it an attitude towards language. Langö can be pursued in two directions: inward, through the letters of the poem, into the deep interior of the poet's soul; or outward, into the world, through the sounding of the text. In the second instance, aesthetic questions focus on congruence between the text (its overt meaning), the sounding of the text (the ways in which it becomes manifest), and its effects on the inner and outer worlds. Old Javanese poems were composed according to distinct metrical patterns, of which over two hundred are known to exist. It is clear that they were intended to be read aloud, and indeed such readings continue today among the "reading clubs" (*sekehe bebasan*) of Bali. These are actually performances in which the most careful attention is paid to both the sounds of the words and their meanings. A reader intones a line from the text, which may have to be repeated if he strays from the correct metrical pattern. Next, another reader proposes a spontaneous translation into modern colloquial Balinese. Once the "meaning" has been tacitly agreed on by all those present, the first reader chants the next line. The Balinese words for these "readings" (*mengidung, mekekawin,* etc.) are, I think best rendered into English as "sounding" the text, in both the sense of turning its letters into sounds and that of searching for its meanings. From this "reading" or "sounding" it is but a short step to performance, where all the devices of music, language and the theater are employed to carry the meaning, the langö into the world. Such performances are powerful—not because of word-magic, but because the more beautiful (alangö) a performance, the more attractive it will be. Sounding the text dispels the illusions of ordinary consciousness and brings to light the underlying structures that bind man and nature, past and present, inner and outer. The events of everyday life are divested of their apparent uniqueness, and people become aware of themselves as acting in accordance with age-old scripts.

The sounding of the texts brings written order into the world, displaying the logos which lies beyond the illusion of mundane existence. Obviously, for this to be effective, the stories told must bear an important resemblance to events in the lives of the hearers or audience. Consequently, it is one of the distinguishing characteristics of serious Balinese drama, shadow-theater, or other "soundings of the text" that the performers must not decide on the story to be told until they have assessed the needs of the audience. Here is Wija, a Balinese shadow-puppeteer, in an interview with an American story-teller, Diane Wolkstein [1979:27]:

WOLKSTEIN: How do you choose which story you will tell?

WIJA: It is always different. Before performance begins we are served coffee and tea by the community or the people who have asked for the wayang. I talk with the people. Very often those who have sponsored the wayang will ask for certain things to be stressed.

WOLKSTEIN: If you go to a village where there are troubles, do you try to solve them?

WIJA: Of course! That is my job! The wayang reflects our life ... Just as the Pandawas are always being tempted by the Kauravas, their enemies, we too are always being tempted by evil. By taking the shadows of the wayang into ourselves, we are strengthened by the struggle and the victory of the Pandawas. The clashing of the swords and the heaving of the divine weapons are only the outer image of the internal battle.

In essence, a wayang performance is analogous to that of a reading club— a "sounding of the text." Line by line, an ancient text is sounded, and then an attempt is made at translation and interpretation. In a reading club, this is done orally, while in a wayang performance, music, puppets and the theatrical skills of the puppeteer are used to enhance the interpretation. The whole performance is structured in such a way as to pose questions about the relationship of the text to those who see and hear it performed. The puppeteer is seated behind a cloth screen, which is illuminated by the flickering light of an oil

A Balinese Topeng dancer performing a *bebali* (performance for both the human and divine audience) at a temple festival.

lamp. Several hundred puppets are employed, representing the gods and heroes of Balinese mythology, inhabitants of the worlds that are ordinarily hidden from human sight by the veil of maya (illusion). The puppets are richly painted, but appear on the audience's side of the screen only as dark shadows, suggesting that the reality of the gods is so brilliant as to be beyond human sight or imagination. The wayang screen is in one sense a window in maya, which allows us to peer into the dazzling world of the gods (for whom *we* are monochromatic shadows). In special wayang performances held for the entertainment of the gods, without a human audience, the screen is not used. The stories must be evoked by puppets speaking accurate Old Javanese; the sounds of their voices, enhanced by music from the wayang orchestra, are intrinsically powerful. Thus, on the Mountain of Poets in East Java, a wayang performance goes on continuously, day and night, sometimes with an audience but often not. The performance itself creates an order in the world, as in the story of the rampaging giant who was finally quieted by the sight of a wayang, which drew him in and made him cease his random destruction.

Before beginning a performance, a puppeteer ritually cleanses himself with holy water, holds the Tree of Life puppet to his forehead, closes his eyes and calls the gods to their places. The puppeteer Wija explains:

> There can be no world without direction. The gods have names and places in the compass. By calling their names, they go to their places—their homes. The last is the east which is the place of birth—the beginning. At this moment, too, the orchestra is playing the sunrise melody. In the wayang the puppeteer is god, and he is asking to be located in his proper place—his center—so that the creation can begin. [Wolkstein 1979:27]

The gods whom he "calls to their places" have their homes equally at the ends of the world and within the self, according to Balinese belief. They are the gods of both the macro- and microcosm (in Balinese, "Great Realm"— *Buana Agung*; and "Small Realm"—*Buana Alit*). The structure of a wayang performance creates a rich and complex metaphor of inner and outer realities. The puppeteer constructs a world of pure illusion, which is paradoxically also the "real" world. Each audience—the gods and the human spectators— appears as a mere shadow to the other. The puppeteer animates the gods who in another sense animate him: gods who rule the "Great Realm" yet are found within himself. These paradoxes of illusion and reality are fully exploited in the wayang, and lead us deeper into the nature of the power Balinese attribute to "sounding the text."

Within the context of Western notions of the "life of texts in the world," it is easy to see that wayang might possess what we might call an "illuminative" function. A well-told tale in a wayang might "instruct" the Balinese audience in essentially the same way that a Biblical parable expounded in a church service is meant to edify a Christian congregation. But wayang performed without an audience, like the endless performance on Poetry Mountain, is more mysterious. The Balinese explanation for such performances is that wayang can *create* order, in both the inner and outer worlds. To create order in the world is the privilege of gods, but the gods themselves are animated shadows in the wayang, whom the puppeteer calls to their places as he assumes the power of creation. It is significant that the effectiveness of wayang does not depend on the audience "really" believing that the puppeteer (or his puppets) are divine. In fact, quite the reverse is true. One of the most popular texts for wayang is the tenth-century poem *Arjuna Wijaya*. In this passage the god Indra, disguised as an elderly human, instructs the hero Arjuna:

> Blinded by the passions and the world of the senses, one fails to acquire knowledge of oneself. For it is as with the spectators of a puppet-performance: they are carried away, cry and are sad (because of what befalls their beloved hero or heroine), in the ignorance of their understanding. And this even though they know that it is merely carved leather that moves and speaks. That is the image of one whose desires are bound to the objects of the senses and who refuses to understand that all appearances are only an illusion and a display of sorcery without any reality. [Zoetmulder 1974]

Yet despite this emphatic disavowal of "magical" powers in the puppets, puppeteers are regarded by the Balinese as a kind of priest. But they are priests whose aim is not to mystify with illusion but to clarify the role of illusion in our perception of reality. As Wija explained, "Wayang means shadow—reflection. Wayang is used to reflect the gods to the people, and the people to themselves." Wayang reveals the power of language and the imagination to go beyond "illumination," to construct an order in the world which exists both in the mind and, potentially, in the outer world as well. The performance itself poses questions, in the minds of the audience, about the relations between imaginary worlds, perceptual worlds, and "real" worlds. In contemplating a wayang, one sees that the boundaries between inner and outer realities—imagined worlds, the world before our eyes, and the world of the past and present which we take to be "real"—are forever shifting and in flux.

Language and Performance

It is characteristic of the sounding of the text in Balinese performances that several different languages are used. Usually, they are juxtaposed—different characters speak in different languages—in order to exploit different properties of language. Balinese libraries house texts in Sanskrit, Old Javanese,

Middle Javanese, Balinese and Indonesian. The first three of these are ancient languages, now spoken only in performances, where they conjure up the worlds of the gods and the splendid kingdoms of the dim past. In Alton Becker's useful phrase, they are languages used for "speaking the past." To "speak the present," one uses Balinese or Indonesian. But spoken Balinese itself is divided into registers which carry distinct connotations of place: High Balinese is courtly language; Middle Balinese is formal speech between equals; Low Balinese, the vernacular of the villages. In the same way, the use of modern Indonesian invokes a modern urban context. As we will see in a moment, all of these languages and registers may be employed in a theatrical performance, allowing a single actor to step adroitly from one historical/linguisitic context to another:

Realm	Language or Register
Modern World	Indonesian
Traditional Villages	Low Balinese
Recent Balinese Courts	High Balinese
Medieval Javanese Kingdoms	Middle Javanese
Legendary Past of "Indian" Epics—Heroic Age	Old Javanese
Timeless Realms of the Gods	Sanskrit

In the following excerpt from the first few minutes of a "mask theater" (*topeng*) performance, a single dancer shifts from language to language (and realm to realm) as he tells the story of the invasion of an East Javanese kingdom by a fifteenth-century Balinese king, Jelantik. [Emigh 1979:38-39]

Excerpt from "Jelantik Goes to Blambangan"
Pensar Kelihan, a clown/servant/storyteller, wearing a purple half-mask with round, bulging eyes, emerges from behind a curtain and begins to dance, to the accompaniment of gamelan music.

Language	Speech
Middle Javanese (excerpt from poem "Kidung Tantri")	A story is told of the King of Patali, rich, proud, and full of dignity. (Dances proudly.) Truly magnificent! Proceeding now! AAaat! Ah! Ha, ha, ha! Arah! Hi, hi, hi!
Old Javanese (excerpt from the Old Javanese version of the Mahabharata—tenth century)	At dawn, the red sun rises. The rustling of leaves on the mountainside joins the sounds of the frogs large and small.
Middle Balinese	I'm so happy! So happy! I never get bored, telling you about my happiness! Like today! Why don't I get bored, talking about my happiness? Ayah! Hi, hi, hi! Heh! Why am I so happy? Because I just now became a bachelor again! Hi, hi, hi!
High Balinese	Oh my lord and king. I try to follow you loyally. I beseech you, lay not your curse upon me, for I am going to tell your story now. Singeh! Singeh! Please! Please! I pay homage to the ancestors, to those who are already holy. And to the divine trinity, the Holy Lords Wisnu, Brahma, and Iswara. And I pay homage as well to all those who would make the countryside peaceful and prosperous here in ancient Bali. I ask for your blessings. I beseech you not to lay your curses upon me.
Middle Balinese	And why? Why do I offer up these prayers? Because I am about to tell you of my Lord, the great King here in Gelgel, Klungkung, the great Dalem Waturrenggong.

Old Javanese (excerpt from the Old Javanese Ramayana)	Spinning round on his tail, the son of Subali rises higher and higher.
Low Balinese (the local dialect of Klungkung, where the performance is being held)	Aduh! What a chase those noblemen in the orchestra gave me! (He refers to the orchestra for this performance.) Now I'm worn out! Already too tired to give you a show! Mind you, I don't mean to criticize. Not just yet! It's my first time here. My first time dancing with these musicians. Their first time playing with me. And I'm very old-fashioned. Just like an old dog. There's not much fur left on my hide and what there is of it is very short. Huh! Moving on!
High Balinese	My Lord and Master, Dalem Waturrenggong, is the ruler of this kingdom. His mind is troubled now, filled with thoughts of His Royal Highness, His Majesty, the King of Blambangan.
Middle Balinese	What could have broken up their old friendship?

In the space of a few minutes, the actor had invoked four languages, of which most of his audience will understand only two or three. He has quoted from both of the great Hindu epics, the Ramayana and the Mahabharata, along with the Middle Javanese court poem, Kidung Tantri. He steps "out of character" for an instant to make fun of himself as a "mangy old dog of a performer," then instantly returns to his role of servant in a sixteenth-century Balinese court. In a manner unknown to Western theater, he weaves a story into the world of the audience and creates connections among the many worlds conjured up by the language and poetry he uses.

Ancestral visitation is ancient in Indonesian cultures, and continues to play a part in many Balinese theatrical performances in the phenomenon called "trance." The spirit of a performer can be "inhabited" by the spirit of the one he portrays. In this sort of drama, the performer always enters from behind a drawn curtain, after first shaking the curtain in such a way as to suggest some Power taking possession of it. There is thus a certain ambiguity about the dramatic figures who emerge from behind the curtain: are they actors, or visiting spirits? John Emigh comments on the entrance of the evil king, in a later episode of the performance quoted above:

> As the King of Blambangan shakes the curtain, thereby cueing a frenzied rush of percussive sound, he cries out in Old Javanese, "Behold, here I come, the King of Blambangan," and warns the audience that preparation is necessary to witness his powerful countenance. The curtain is yanked open and the King thrusts his animalistic hands forward, looking through the opened curtain into the performance oval, demanding to know whom it is he is facing. Is he talking to the warriors from Gelgel who have invaded his territory? Or is he speaking to the audience he sees revealed to him in a language which is no longer theirs? The ambiguity is deliberate. By shifting back and forth between modes of illusion and visitation, the performer can playfully toy with the vantage point of the audience. [Ibid.]

The ability of different languages to evoke different "realms" is part of the reason why so many languages are employed in the theater. But from a Balinese perspective, differences between languages go deeper than their association with a particular time and place. Different languages are regarded as having different properties and hence different constraints on their use. Sanskrit and Old Javanese, the languages used to "speak the past," are intrinsically powerful and may not be lightly used. The nature of this power has been investigated by several scholars, beginning with C.C. Berg, who drew attention to passages in Old Javanese texts such as the *Hariwangsa*, which state the author's desire to promote, by the words of the text, "the invincibility of the king and the prosperity of the world." Following Berg, Zoetmulder observed that certain languages may create such effects because "there is a kind of identity between the word and what it stands for. But the degree of its effectiveness is dependent on various factors. It is high if the words are taken from a text or are borrowed from a language that is considered sacred" [1974:167].

In modern semiology, this would be described as an iconic view of language. Michel Foucault has ascribed a similar view of language to sixteenth-century Europe:

> In its original form, when it was given to men by God himself, language was an absolutely certain and transparent sign for things, because it resembled them. The names of things were lodged in the things they designated, just as strength is written in the body of the lion, regality in the eye of the eagle, just as the influence of the planets is marked upon the brows of men: by form of similitude. This transparency was destroyed at Babel as a punishment for men. Languages became separated and incompatible with one another only insofar as they had previously lost this original resemblance to things that had been the prime reason for the existence of language. [1970:36]

Thus, according to Foucault, in the "classical" sixteenth-century view, language lost its direct iconic nature at the Tower of Babel. For this reason, the oldest language (Hebrew), while no longer directly connected with the things it names, still contains, "as if in the form of fragments, the marks of that original name-giving." This seems very close to the Balinese view, that Sanskrit is close to being a "perfect" language, in the sense that the connection between the word and what it signifies is not seen as arbitrary but intrinsic. Compare Foucault's example of this iconic view of language with Zoetmulder's:

> FOUCAULT: Paracelsus asks, "Tell me, then, why snakes in Helvetia, Algoria, Swedland understand the Greek words Osy, Osya, Osy... In what academies did they learn them, so that scarcely have they heard the word than they immediately turn tail in order not to hear it again? Scarcely do they hear the word, when, notwithstanding their nature and their spirit, they remain immobile and poison no one." [1970:33]

> ZOETMULDER (quoting Old Javanese texts): "Whosoever listens devotedly (*tuhagana*) to the story of Astika and the serpent-sacrifice has no need to fear serpents." [1974:166]

For the Balinese, certain Sanskrit slokas possess this iconicity and are therefore "magical." Sanskrit is also supposed to be the oldest language. More recent languages—Old Javanese, Middle Javanese, Balinese, Indonesian—are less and less iconic, but the power of Old and Middle Javanese poetry resides in no small part in its iconicity, and for this reason, the manner of its "sounding" is critical for its efficacy.

Iconicity is dramatically portrayed as a possibility in texts such as the Old Javanese Ramayana, in which powerful words spoken by a character with sufficient *sakti* (power) *must* happen. But it is not only the language in which the words are spoken but the circumstance of their utterance that makes the words come true. Sanskrit is the most iconic—the meaning of a mantra cannnot be realized if it is not sounded correctly and in the proper circumstances. On the other hand, words spoken in Indonesian or modern Balinese cannot be iconic under any circumstances. Thus, it is only in the total context of a performance that the issue of the relationship of a symbol to its referent can be settled. For an articulate Balinese, language can seemingly take on any resonance, from a sound which echos music and is the true name of a thing, to words rich with archaic associations and social connotations, to mere weightless, arbitrary signs.

This suggests an important difference between the Western and Balinese attitudes toward the relationship of a particular language to the world. Foucault poses this question in an interesting way in the concept of the *episteme*: the principles of linguistic order, or classification, which establish preconditions for systems of knowledge. For Foucault there is no order,

> no similitude and no distinction, even for the wholly untrained perception, that is not the result of a precise operation and of the application of a preliminary criterion. A "system of elements"— a definition of the segments by which those segments can be affected, and lastly, the threshold above which there is a difference and below which there is a similitude—is indispensible for the establishment of even the simplest form of order. [1970:xx]

In *The Order of Things*, Foucault examines for post-medieval European culture "what modalities of order have been recognized, posited, linked with space and time, in order to create the positive basis of knowledge as we find it employed in grammar and philology, in natural history and biology, in the study of wealth and political economy."

Foucault traces the succession of epistemes as a linear process, in which one episteme succeeds another. Thus, in his view, "classical" thought crumbled at the end of the eighteenth-century when language ceased utterly to be iconic, and "words wandered off on their own." Foucault shares with Derrida a perception that the "modernity" of our thought is based on our discovery of language—our sense of language as the "empty play of signifiers." Foucault's perception of a linear succession of epistemes in Western culture, each ultimately grounded in a different linguistic order, provides a clear contrast to the relationship of language to culture in Bali. Here languages and textual traditions do not succeed one another; rather they coexist and interact with one another. In the space of a few minutes, as we saw in the excerpt from "Jelantik Goes to Blambangan," a Balinese actor can employ the different properties of several languages to construct, in the minds of the audience, several distinct "realms" or realities. It is precisely the juxtaposition of different realms—or in Foucault's terminology, epistemes—that creates the drama. The plot of a "story" is secondary, almost unimportant; theatrical tension is created by the interaction of the "imaginary" realms with the present situation of the audience. Because stories must not be chosen beforehand, the challenge for performers is to bring the different textual traditions of the past to bear on the novelties of the present, molding them into continuing patterns of order.

Clowns, Music, and the Boundaries of Time

We have seen that the different languages of Bali are each associated with a different realm, and that these realms are arranged in a sort of chronological order, from the ancient times to the present. It has also been hinted that in the context of dramatic performances, different languages are often associated with different musical styles. This association of music with language may seem somewhat foreign to us, but from the standpoint of Balinese aesthetics,

A Balinese Brahmin reading from a lontar manuscript.

the sounding of words and music are intimately related. Music is never merely ornamental; it is an integral part of the process by which the boundaries between the worlds are made permeable. The sounds of powerful words are mingled with the flow of music, which has the power to shape and bend time itself, in the minds of the hearers. The flow of sounds creates a tempo, a perceived rhythm of time. Thus, as the texts are sounded, performers and even members of the audience are caught up in the flow, experiencing sounds to which they fit their movements, their thoughts, ultimately perhaps their whole perception. Obviously this is not only a Balinese phenomenon; it is the common human experience of music. But Balinese aesthetics emphasizes the power of music to shape people's perceptions, particularly of time and temporal rhythms. For the Balinese, absorption in the flow of sounds can finally be total, leading to a state of "trance" in which one is "in" the music-time or music-world. This is not simply a passive state of musical rapture, the absorption in the sounds alone that comes with listening attentively to a good performer. It is, or rather it is described by the Balinese as being, an active experience of being *in* the music-world, the other-world. This is possible because the sounds of the music and the text are iconic for one another, and both point to a particular imaginary world. The music-world *is* the place spoken of in the text and portrayed by the dancers or puppets. Watching a performance on an admittedly rather bare and tatty stage or wayang screen, one is nonetheless carried along by the flow of sounds to lose oneself amid the images of the myths.

As Judith Becker has recently shown, the flow of music is the basic metaphor in Balinese thought for the flow of time. The Balinese conceptualize time not in terms of a linear flow, but rather as many repeating cycles, which reflect the rhythms of growth of the natural world. Calendars depict the intersections of different cycles, or weeks. In a Balinese gamelan orchestra, each musician plays a cyclical, repetitive piece, and the fabric of the melody is created by the interlocking of the various cycles. Becker explains: "The fundamental governing principle in gamelan music is the cyclical recurrence of a melodic/temporal unit, which is a musical manifestation of the way in which the passage of time is also ordered" [1974:198]. The intersection of cycles gives time, as well as music, a kind of texture. Each day has a meaning, a quality, according to where it falls in the intersection of several cycles. This concept is essentially foreign to Western calendars, although we do have a single example: Friday the Thirteenth, a special kind of day, with a quality inherent in its position at the juncture of two cycles. By showing the qualities of different intersecting cycles, Balinese calendars tell, as Clifford Geertz put it, "not what time it is, but what *kind* of time it is." These cycles are not arbitrary units, but are regarded as expressing the true rhythms of time. According to Balinese cosmology, every living being is on its own temporal or developmental cycle, a process of growth followed by decay. Events occur as cycles touch, when beings interact with one another in the "Middle World." In this way, past and present, man and nature are not separated, but woven together: "The forest feels dejected in the month of Asadha, because its chill makes poets shiver and even sick from cold."

But in the theater, there are special characters who alone are immune to the cycles of time—characters who move across the boundaries of time, music, and language. These characters are of special interest because they are not mentioned in any of the ancient texts, but play an important part nonetheless in the telling of most stories. They are called *parekan*, a word usually translated into English as "clowns" or "fools," and they are indeed bumbling, odd-shaped, buffoonish creatures who play the role of servants to the gods and heroes of the stories. Their chief function appears to be one of translation: when it seems likely that members of the audience do not understand part of the story (probably because they do not understand the language being used, for few Balinese are fluent in all the languages of the theater), the clowns step in, translating and interpreting, making jokes, and rendering everything into Low Balinese.

The function of these clowns poses an interesting problem about the relationship of the text to the audience. In one sense, they bring the drama to the audience as helpful translators. But their function as translators could easily be obviated by translating the text itself, as we perform Aeschylus in modern English. The structural effect of retaining the clowns is really the reverse: to create a space between the world of the audience and the text as it is invoked onstage. The clowns create a liminal space for themselves, and they play with the structures that create the boundaries of the performance: music, language, and dramatic style. Mediating between performers and audience, they speak to themselves, to the audience, and to the mythical characters who speak the words of the ancient texts. Like all clowns, they have no social position and are therefore free to comment on the social dramas they observe. We might think of them as cousins to Shakespeare's fools—except that in Shakespeare, the clowns never speak directly to the audience, though they are forever trying to instill a reflexive awareness in their lords and masters, as the Fool does for Lear.

But what distinguishes Balinese clowns from those of the European tradition is their power of translation—the power to control the sounding of the text. Dancing back and forth between performers and audience, translating and enhancing some words while allowing others to pass into the void, they create the channels for the sounding of the text. In this sense, they are the masters of poesis—the use of words to create poetic worlds which are more true, more real than the everyday waking world of the audience.

That the Balinese recognize this power as supreme is shown in the worst-kept secret of the Balinese theater, the identity of the greatest of clowns, Twalen. Twalen is the prince of fools, a fat Falstaffian buffoon who usually plays the servant of the godlike Pandawas. But in reality, as everyone knows, Twalen is the elder brother of Siva, greatest of the gods, and is thus older and more powerful that all the gods.

Conclusion

One of the major trends in post-structualist semiotics has been a progressive distancing of the author, and the reader, from the text. In part, this derives from an early emphasis, in structural linguistics, on viewing languages as systems of signs, autonomous in the sense that they may be understood without reference to the minds of the speaker or hearer, writer or reader. More recently, this view of language has been challenged. Chomsky's argument that language must be understood in relation to mind, helped to inaugurate a post-structuralist phase in linguistics. Few linguists now see language from a strictly Sausseurean perspective, as an "autonomous" system of signs.

Separation of language and mind has also been strongly challenged from an evolutionary, biological perspective. Increasingly studies of the role of language in the brain suggest that language and thought are inextricably linked and that the origin of human (as distinct from animal) language does not lie in social communication. For that purpose, according to most researchers, a much simpler language consisting of a few hundred signs would be ample. Harry J. Jerison provides a persuasive summary of research on the evolution of symbolic language in the human line:

> If there were selection pressures toward the development of language specifi-

cally for communication, we would expect the evolutionary response to be the development of "prewired" language systems with conventional sounds and symbols. These are the typical approaches to communication in other vertebrates, and they are accomplished (as in birds) with little or no learning and with relatively small neural systems. The very flexibility and plasticity of the language systems of the human brain argue for their evolution as having been analogous to that of other sensory integrative systems, which are now known to be unusually plastic, or modifiable by early experience. (Benjamin Lee Whorf and Edward Sapir pointed this out many years ago as one of the maladaptive features of this flexibility of the language system, which enables different societies to develop different languages and hence different realities, often with catastrophic effects on the interactions of human communities.)

I am proposing here that the role of language in communication first evolved as a side effect of its basic role in the perception of reality. The fact that communication is so central to our present view of language does not affect the argument. It is, in fact, theoretically elegant to explain the evolution of an important novel adaptation in a species by relating it to the conversion of earlier patterns of adaptation. We can think of language as being merely an expression of another neural contribution to the construction of mental imagery, analogous to the contributions of the encephalized sensory systems and their association systems. *We need language more to tell stories than to direct action.* [2] In the telling we create mental images in our listeners that might normally be produced only by the memory of events as recorded and integrated by the sensory and perceptual systems of the brain…. In hearing or reading another's words, we literally share another's consciousness, and it is that familiar use of language that is unique to man.

Language, then, is far more than a colorless medium of communication, more even than a system of signs—for it plays a continuous active role in the processes of imagining and interpreting the world. It is from this perspective

2. Emphasis mine.—J.S.L.

on language that we can appreciate the richness of the Southeast Asian concept of "sounding the text." It is in the mind that the flow of sounds—music and language—can join with visual images, even shadows, in the process Rothenberg has called "world-making and self-making." The power to control the sounding of the text, as Twalen shows us, is the power to create the world.

References Cited

Becker, Alton and Yengoyan, Aram, eds., *The Imagination of Reality: Essays in Southeast Asian Coherence Systems.* Norwood, N.J.: Ablex, 1979.

Foucault, Michel, *The Order of Things (Les Mots et les Choses).* New York: Pantheon, 1970.

Harari, Josue, ed., *Textual Strategies: Perspectives in Post-Structuralist Criticism.* Ithaca: Cornell University Press, 1979.

Jerison, Harry J., *Evolution of the Brain and Intelligence.* Academic Press, 1973.

Rasmussen, David, *Mythic-Symbolic Language and Philosophical Anthropology.* The Hague: Nijhoff, 1971.

Stapel, F.W., *Geschiedenis van Nederlandsch-Indie.* Amsterdam, 1938.

Tobias, Philip V., *The Brain in Hominid Evolution.* New York: Columbia University Press, 1971.

Wolkstein, Diane, "Master of the Shadow Play," *Parabola*, Vol. IV No. 4, 1979.

Zoetmulder, P.J., *Kalangwan, A Survey of Old Javanese Literature.* The Hague: Nijhoff, 1974.

DAVID GUSS

Reading the Mesa:
An Interview with
Eduardo Calderón

EDUARDO CALDERÓN PALOMINO is a *curandero* from the Trujillo area of Northern Peru, a region famous for its practitioners of the healing arts. Common to the practice of *curanderismo* in this area is the use of a *mesa*, an altarlike assemblage of "artifacts" arranged in various fields of power. With the aid of chants and a hallucinogen made from the San Pedro cactus, these artifacts are manipulated during the healing ceremony in order to give the *curandero* the *cuenta* or "account" necessary to diagnose his patient. This "account," transpiring between the *curandero* and his *mesa*, is a psychic reading that depends on the healer's ability to locate the appropriate "artifact" through which the spirit will speak.

Every *curandero*'s *mesa* is unique. Eduardo's is divided into three fields: that of the right, the *Campo Justiciero*, "the Field of the Divine Judge"; that of the middle, the *Campo Medio*, the mediating "Field of San Cyprian"; and that of the left, the *Campo Ganadero*, "the Field of Satan," also known as "the Field of the Sly Dealer." Carefully arranged on these three fields are more than seventy artifacts that include, among other things, shells, stones, crystals, rattles, daggers, tobacco, pre-Columbian shards, post-Conquest *santos*, and bottles of herbs, perfumes, and holy water. Ringing the back of the *mesa* is a row of staffs and swords which Eduardo refers to as the antennae that help transmit the "accounts." The attention of the séance is on balancing the energies of these different fields. Only in this way can the patient also regain the "balance of power" which is at the very center of Eduardo's philosophy of healing.

In reading about him and hearing him speak, it occurred to me that Eduardo used his *mesa* like a gigantic book to which he turned for the "accounts,"

needed to diagnose his patients. The artifacts were the pages or chapters of this book and as he himself claimed: "Each artifact has a story, and each story is basically equated with the request of each individual, with each patient, which is wrapped up in it." I had an opportunity to discuss these ideas with Eduardo in June of 1981 when he visited California. He had been flown up from Peru by Douglas Sharon to participate in a conference on shamanism at the San Diego Museum of Man. After the conference, Eduardo came to L.A., where he spoke to a small group in a seminar room at UCLA on a Thursday evening. When the talk ended several of us stayed on, and I asked Eduardo what he thought about "reading the *mesa*" as a book. Mick Taussig was there, visiting from Michigan. So was Doug Sharon and a graduate student named Molly Doty. The following are some excerpts from the interview, which took place in Spanish and which I subsequently translated.

For his generous aid in facilitating this interview and then later in going over its transcription, I am grateful to Doug Sharon. I am also grateful to Lydia Degarrod (& her wonderful ears!) for helping me with the initial transcription. For more information about Eduardo Calderón and his ideas about healing, one should see Douglas Sharon's *Wizard of the Four Winds: A Shaman's Story* (The Free Press, N.Y., 1978) as well as the film *Eduardo the Healer*, produced by Douglas Sharon and distributed by Audio Visual Services, Pennsylvania State University, Special Services Building, 1127 Fox Hill Road, University Park, PA 16803-1824.

DAVID GUSS: And that's why we were thinking that, in that sense, the *mesa* is like a book too. That it's a space, a sacred space, which when you were talking about the *mesa*, it sounded like a book, no?, which actually has its own tales, and which, in a way, you read, no?, like one reads chapters....

EDUARDO CALDERÓN: Yes, of course, from that point of view it would be like giving a reading, no?, in which the *mesa* would be, would become, like a book which is read in oriental style from right to left, using or conveying the rhythmic cycle of expression, of conduct, or rather, that which is today to that which was, and that which was to that which is today—always following a cyclical rhythm. Each "account" belongs, let's say, to a stage, a stage which is equated with, for example, which you have to balance with your basic center of action, with…with the other page, which you have to also connect with. Which is to say, everything is based on connections and nothing else. Connections at the level of ideas, mental ideas which are balanced to give a simple result. Now, what is that result? It's the truth, the important point, the logical balance of a cure, of something, something which you hope to know, which you hope, let's say, to receive in order to balance yourself, and nothing more.

DG: And it seems like everything you do is a way of reading it, such as the chanting, taking San Pedro...

EC: Exactly. Each chant is a determined point of action which is linked to a request, to a concern of each patient. It's the same as in the Bible where there's an important concern in *The Song of Songs*, in the *Psalms*, in those where, for example, they predict something already written which is going to happen. But this responds to each person, to each individual, to each sensation…projecting, accenting his essence, no? his philosophy. Each man is a world. And that world is balanced in accord with the understanding of what the symbols mean. [Raising his glass] Salud.

DOUG SHARON: And the "accounts," compadre? What role do they play in the book? What is it?

EC: The "accounts" would become nothing less than the basic record. It's like a person, from his birth until the present moment, he makes a regressive action by way of the important points of his life—going backward, and going forward. In the field of the "account" of this book which could be called the *mesa*, it would come point by point.

This action, which is to say, this dynamic, the dynamic of this book at the level of "accounts," would be like a rosary as used by a priest or a mystic in order not to jump off the spot, always repeating the cycle.

Each artifact has a story, and each story is basically equated with the request of each individual, with each patient, which is wrapped up in it. As much in the *Campo Justiciero* ("the Field of the Divine Judge") as in the *Campo Medio* ("the Middle Field," "the Field of San Cyprian") and the *Campo Ganadero* ("the Field of the Sly Dealer," "the field of Satan"). Harmonization! In the sense that this, with this you have to balance at an elemental, at a bio-electric magnetic level, that opposition of forces, at a balanced level, and nothing less. The chants, the music, the melody are all in agreement with that sense of harmony of the individual …with each "account." The "account" of love then has a type of sound, a type of hiss, of song, of music, and goes with each offering (the *prenda*, or article of clothing), each artifact, each element which is on the *mesa*.

DG: When a person comes then, you have to know what the "account" for that person is?

EC: Yes. She comes out in front. Okay. The diagnosis is the result of the inducement of the energy particular to the master and the control panel, in order to see *at what point it is, on what page it's found* [swishing sound of turn-

ing pages]. And one begins to evoke, to, let's say, to state the problematic.

D G : In that sense it has all the "accounts"; it's an infinite book.

E C : It's an infinite book. Yes, exactly, an infinite book.

D G : One thinks of it in a biblical sense, then, as the Bible is said to contain everything.

E C : Exactly. A man is a book. Each man is a book. But that book is a particular one, in the sense that when all the books are balanced together they form the universal book.

MICHAEL TAUSSIG: (wistfully) When will that be? (laughter)

D G : Sceptical, huh?

M T : Just hoping.

EC: Well, exactly. Hope is one of the factors of the... let's say, which is equated with the mystic symbolism of the, of the amphora of Pandora, for example. It was opened up and the only thing left was hope... and something else, no?
   (laughter)
Well, anything else you wanted to ask?

MT: Something else about this I'd like to ask. Okay. Each man and woman is a book, no? But this story, this tale, this book can be obvious or very obscure, no? I imagine that with a sick person, his tale, for example, his book is badly written, or it's obscure?

EC: His book is an imbalance. Or rather, there may have been a stain, or a blot made at the level of action. But it's clear that you can go over it again.

MT: Through...?

EC: Right.

MT: Then, it's like a pencil too, no?

EC: It's like a pencil. You make an error and you go back to re-balance, or rather, simply to a level of balance. If I know I write something, and an accident, an event, a problem happens in this field, then I go back again to balance myself, to reconnect myself with this thing. In life the individual can either march into chaos or step back into semichaos and re-balance himself, taking off again on a new path. That's what we're looking for in the question of therapy, psychotherapy: that the individual doesn't break, doesn't unravel his ties. If not, on the other hand, he can connect himself again and begin travelling on the path which is right for him, without stumbling. The paths are many, and one can't travel on all of them. And, in that philosophical sense, man is infinite.

MOLLY DOTY: Is one born with this book already made?

E C : The books are there. The pages are open. What happens is that one has to lay the type, put in the type.

M T : Mom and Dad, start writing!
   (laughter)

E C : If these ideas were taken into account at a general level in every mind, what an awakening, no? Hmm, how would that be, no? We would be in a great advance. But while some sleep, others are so awake, others don't want to wake up and others refuse to wake up; and others don't much give a damn in the end! That's the problem. You have to be every minute: "Tch, tch, tch, tch. Tch, tch, tch, tch [the rapid sound of knocking]. *Despiertate*! Wake up! *Oiga!* Listen! Swsh, swsh, swsh. Swsh, swsh" [the sound of a hand whistling through the air like someone gently slapping a face for attention]. And no one wants to wake up, huh? And so the Awakener: "Rhumm, rhumm" [a deep revving, charging sound]. They throw him on the floor. They cover him up. And that's the problem, that people don't want to wake up.

   And you've got to use great strength, sometimes sacrifices, in order to wake up. Oh, sometimes an awakening comes, suddenly, no? Oh, and, "Is this reality or is this nothing?" Then…or, "Is it conscious or an advance?" And if not, he leaves it. When he realizes it, it's too late. Because now he's gone too far and he has to turn around and go back. And sometimes he doesn't want to go back. He doesn't want to. "Ahhh," he says, "I'll go." Always with the hope he's going to find it.

   Down whatever road you go…you're going, you're going, let's say, you're reharmonizing again, but it's very difficult.

   Chance, you see but one time…hmmm…maximum two times. But a third time she won't enter. They say that Chance, for example, is a woman without eyes, with one hair, one single hair, and with wings on her feet, and she enters by the window, never passing throught the door. Yes, that's the way she is.

   And you've got to heed the knock. And if she leaves, shh, forget it!

KARL YOUNG

Bookforms

I MAKE BOOKS. I publish trade editions under the Membrane Press imprint. I also make facsimilies of indigenous-style Mexican manuscripts, and of screenfolds and scrolls based on Oriental models. For a number of years I have been working on a series of one-of-a-kind books; photographs of some of them are presented here. In this series I have been trying to produce new bookforms or introduce new materials into the spinebound format that dominates all contemporary western book design and manufacture. Most of the photographs are of books that fall into the second category: the books are covered with wrappers and their pages, bound along a spine, are not sheets of paper but metal printing plates, dollar bills, pieces of wood, concrete blocks, etc. In some cases the size of the pages alone removes them from the dominant notion of what a book is—this is the case with the books that can be worn as earings and those whose front and back covers can be brought together, producing a radiant, implied cylinder. Some have been designed for specific purposes other than what most people would consider normal reading. Books whose pages are wooden blocks or resonating chambers, sometimes filled with materials that rattle when shaken, are meant to be used as musical instruments and were made for specific performance artists or for my own use in specific performances.

Book worn as earring.

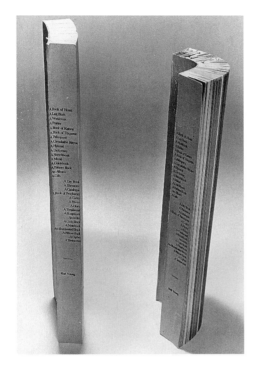

Books with tall, thin pages—made to be folded into several forms, such as cylinders.

Fifth Series: Pornography. Pages made from pages of pornographic magazines. The book is bound on three sides and can only be opened slightly along one edge.

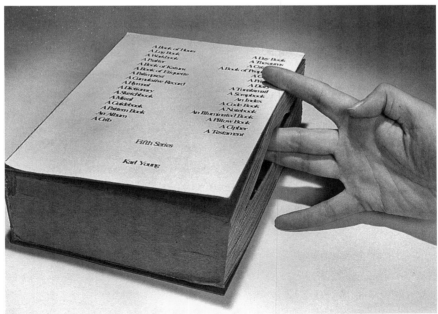

Another source for the present series has been my interest in the history of book design and manufacture, which probably, in turn, comes from my bookmaking activities. Most important have been the books of East Asia and pre-Conquest Mexico, though other forms, like the inlaid books of Southeast Asia, the tablets of Mesopotamia, the quipus of the Andes, and the hand-painted books of medieval Europe have also suggested possibilities. Of course, this interest, too, has informed my more conventional books.

My aims in producing the present series have been relatively simple: to throw out forms, perhaps for future use, but basically in the spirit of invention; to insist that the bookform that dominates our culture is not the only possiblility—we have other options, even if we try to ignore them; to suggest that a book is not merely something whose lines you silently drag your eyes across, but something that can make music, that can involve you in performance and even magic (the first books, aside from simple lists and tallies, were probably more ceremonial implements than data storage systems). Although I'm serious in making these books, I also want them to be amusing to the people who encounter them. This is, in effect, part of the previously mentioned goal: though I want to present alternatives, I don't think they need be solemn or grim.

I do all production (except for some of the camera work) myself on the Membrane Press books. My involvement with the various processes of book manufacture has been a major source of ideas for books in the present series. The pages of the first set of books I made in this series were sheets of paper that had been fed through the press on numerous occasions (to establish register, correct inking problems, etc.): I had, in effect, produced chance-generated collages in the normal printing process, and making books out of them was simply a matter of determining sequences of pages and binding them together. The pages of the second set of books were blotter sheets used to clean the press—sheets which were deeply dyed with the ink they had removed. This sort of involvement in the printing process has, in turn, had a profound effect on how I write more conventional poetry and how I design Membrane Press books: a good deal of my visual poetry and book designs have originated in the process of bookmaking.

Books used in performances of Jackson Mac Low's *Stanzas for Iris Lezak*. Pages made of two-by-fours. Texts from Mac Low's *Stanzas* and from a similar work of my own.

Performance book for The Four Horsemen. Each page is in effect a box made with quarter-inch plywood, containing marbles, ball bearings, grains, beans, screws, etc. It can make two types of sound: the clapping of pages together and the rattling of the contents of each page–both types of sound may be produced together... All texts are visible in this photograph–appearing only on the edges of the pages. Each line is associated with one of the four members of the group.

Performance book for The Four Horsemen, a sound poetry performance group. Pages made of unfinished two-by-fours. Texts taken from their *Canadada* album, printed densely in many colors.

Performance book for The Four Horsemen. Pages made of two-by-fours covered with felt. Text reads: "HORSES'/HOOVES/COURSE/PROVES/SOURCE/ MOVES/DISCOURSE/DISPROVES/HOARSE/HOOVES."

A Book of Nocturns. Pages made of wooden two-by-fours covered with dark blue and black felt. Texts in white. The book is meant to be used to perform its texts: clap the book once after each line, twice after each stanza. An assistant claps another book, like the one for Mac Low's *Stanzas,* at the end of each poem. Has something of the character of a Japanese Noh play.

Above: *A Book of Nocturns* being performed.

What the Popul Vuh Tells about Itself

Six fragments from the Popol Vuh or "Council Book," translated from the Mayan language known as Quiché.

1. Between 1554 and 1558, members of the former ruling house of the kingdom of the Quiché Maya wrote a book near the ruins of their ancient capital, in the Guatemalan highlands. Missionaries taught them to write the Quiché language in roman characters, and they chose to use this knowledge to rewrite a Book that had come into their world long before the Book of the missionaries. The first words of their work are these:

> This is the beginning of the prior word, here in this place called Quiché.
> Here we shall inscribe, we shall implant the prior word,
> the potential and source for everything done
> in the town of Quiché, in the nation of the Quiché people.

2. The authors, who remain anonymous, speak of their condition as writers, giving the names and epithets of the hieroglyphic book that preceded their own writing, a book that was an *ilb'al*, an "instrument for seeing," like a crystal, eyeglasses, or a telescope (all called *ilb'al* today). When they refer to the hidden reader of the original book, they may be referring to themselves:

> We shall write this now amid the preaching of God, in Christendom now,
> we shall bring it out now because there is no longer a way to see
> The Council Book, a way to see

"The Light that Came from Beside the Sea," an account of
"Our Darkness," a way to see
"The Dawn of Life," as it is called.
There is the original book and ancient writing,
but the reader, interpreter has a secret identity.
Great is his rendition and account
of the lighting of all the sky/earth:
the fourfold marking, fourfold cornering, measuring, fourfold staking,
halving the cord, stretching the cord in the sky, on the earth:
the four markers, the four corners, so to speak,
by the maker, modeler,
mother/father of life, of humankind,
giver of breath, giver of heart,
bearer, upbringer in light, in kinship,
of those who are born in the light, begotten in the light,
caretaker, knower of everything, whatever there is:
sky/earth, lake/sea.

3. The "original book" may have come from somewhere on or near the east coast of Yucatán. It was brought to the Guatemalen highlands by an early generation of Quiché lords, who obtained it in an eastern city, probably the place whose ruins, in Honduras, are known today as Copán, here called Rushes and Riddles:

Then, from beside the sea, they brought it back,
the writing of Rushes, the writing of Riddles.
They spoke of their investiture in their signs, their words.

4. Long before the pilgrimage to the eastern city, in the time of the first motherfathers—the first human works, human designs—there was no need of an instrument for seeing:

They saw all and knew all,
everything under the sky was in view,
the moment they turned around and looked around in the sky, on the earth,
everything was seen without any obstacle.
At first they didn't have to walk around to see what was under the sky—
they just stayed where they were when they looked.
Their knowledge thickened,
they saw through trees, through rocks,
through lakes, through seas, through mountains, through plains.
Truly they were gifted people....
They saw all the way to the four markers, the four corners
in the sky, on the earth.

5. The builders, the sculptors were displeased when their works, their designs said, "We have understood everything great and small," and so:

They were blinded as the face of a mirror is breathed upon,
their vision was blurred,
now they could only see close by, just as far as what was obvious.

6. It was the writings of Reeds and Riddles that overcame the human condition of nearsightedness:

They knew whether war would occur,
everything they saw was clear to them.
Whether death or hunger or conflict would occur,
they simply knew it.
And there was a way to see it, there was a book:
"Council Book" was their name for it.

A revised edition of Dennis Tedlock's complete translation is available from Simon & Schuster.

BECKY COHEN

The Book as an Instrument of Performance

Preface: Some Notes, in Conversation

1. The book as an instrument of performance.

2. Making the text "visible" by gesture and speech, making it alive in a different way than reading it silently to oneself would make it.

3. The book as an extension of the poet's body and voice; held at arm's length or cradled / anchored in the palm, set down against the lap or table, turning leaves, swaying with the book, the book in motion, quick or gentle as the poet voices it.

4. The book as emblem: like the bardic poets with their lyres, the tribal poets beating drums or rattles as their sign of office, the poets here work with their books: a silent instrument for a new voicing.

   The poet's eye in concentration on the instrument at rest: an act of "reading."

5. The particularity of the individual poets simultaneous with the commonality of the task: eighteen poets all with their mouths open: in the sign of breath and song. Poets assembled like a chorus.

6. A confirmation that human beings are their most genuinely innocent and unselfconsciously beautiful when they are working.

7. The occasion for these photographs: not large and public but in a series of private meetings between photographer and poet. She is in search for something archetypal and hidden in the present moment: her invisibility beside their presence.

Becky Cohen
Jerome Rothenberg

List of Participants

William Everson
Michael McClure
Lyn Hejinian
Michael Palmer
Fernando Alegria
Steve McCaffery
Michael Davidson
Robert Duncan
Jackson Mac Low
Leslie Scalapino
Clayton Eshleman
Howard Norman
Laura Chester
David Meltzer
Barbara Einzig
Rae Armantrout
David Guss
Jerome Rothenberg

(in order of appearance)

Photographs © Becky Cohen

statements
an indictment
a criminal prosecution

capable of drawing   painting

the art of painting,
as if painted, as in a painting,
of   for writing, suited for writing
for description

a stile for writing
a needle for embroidering,
embroidery

to scratch, scrape, graze
having scratched
to represent by
lines drawn, to delineate, draw, paint

to express by written characters, to write   to write
name   to inscribe
to write down
to set him down

to
register, enrol
to write down
to propose, move
to move that …;
to write for oneself   for one's own use
note down
to indict   for

the prosecutors

denounce   *to be*

indicted

the articles of

the indictment

the penalty

named in the indictment
named in the indictment

to indict

MORPHEME   1: a bitter crystalline addictive narcotic base   2: the god of dreams   3: a branch of linguistic analysis salvaged without cell proliferation

PHONE   1: a speech sound considered as a physical event without regard to its place in the structure of a language   2: the history and theology of sound changes in a language or revolving vibration   3: a ringing in the ears through holes in the air

[*note* PHONE in Greek designates "a sound, tone" most specifically "the voice, mostly of men," and "a battle cry," "discrepant by the time of a breath"]

On The Book of Bean

The First Guided Tour through The Book of Bean

So here it is to begin at the beginning (but one may also turn to the left and begin at the end). Passing through the soybean endpapers one steps up and through the truck tire inner tube to swing out over the lake, a water reflection of oneself. In page three and four is the bean world of word and letter: a roll deck of alphabetically compiled information, books by Beans and a graffiti panel of the word "bean" from Arabic to Swahili. An eye-level gallery exhibits beans and shoes. All this time and throughout one hears the tape: first the sounds of the carpenter climbing the steps of the Franklin Furnace to go to work, of the Hudson River falls, of feet walking along a path by the water. Then the sounds of the pages being made out of town. There is a horse munching and a morning chicken. This side of the tape is overlaid with a telephone book poem of people named Bean, answered by the name of a real bean legume. ("Scarlet Runner," for example, duets with "Bean, Adelaide.") A bean orchestra is heard: red, black and white beans are sounded in containers of glass, wood and ceramic. (Beans don't all sound the same.) These sounds collage with the reader in real time as he makes his way through the pages. A tunnel exists from the bean in word/letter environment. It is another circle but going the opposite way. It leads the reader to the soup via a bean walking tray.
[1] In the next space, a moonlight kitchen, are the four guides on the trip, the Red Queen and the White Rabbit from Tenniel *Alice*, a Bean God, and a four-headed demon dog. The Bean God is kept out of the house, a Japanese house,

The Book of Bean was Alison Knowles' assemblage installation in the form of a large walk-through book.

by throwing beans in his face at the New Year. These guides have come to steal the soup! The soup space is also the performance area of the book; a large white half circle repeats the moon and provides a stage for performance. Old umbrellas and abandoned clothing have been bunched and burned to make a hill for the running guides. (All objects and garments were found during the summer of the Book building.) There are beans here to be walked on, rolled in or eaten. Beans feel good. The atmosphere is ominous, however, and one is glad for the soup. To continue through, one goes outside the pages and from this vantage sees into the core of the spine. The electrical outlets and tape recorder are visible by turning back a swivel page. Sitting down in page nine we find a "real" book, *Bean Culture*, [2] by a Mr. Sevey. Mr. Sevey purports to present the first book printed in America dealing with the science of bean planting. One can easily escape into admiration of steel engravings of bean harvesters from the early 1900's. The reader leaves via a ladder or out the

window and through a muslin panel printed with contradictory wisdom concerning beans and dreaming. At this last entrance/exit, small soundmaking objects scrape the floor. One can begin again either by going on or turning back. There is a free-standing page in the vicinity of *The Book of Bean*. It is the same size (four by eight feet) as the bound pages; it is made of red pockets and is a notation panel for performance. Duets for a single bean and an object are presented on slips of paper and tags. The objects and ideas are easily taken away. A formal performance accompanies the opening of the book from the white half-circle stage. Real soup is served.

1. All beans in the book were donated by Goya Foods, Inc.
2. Gift of Michael Cooper.

Above: Detail from *The Book of Bean*.

Opposite: Page 5. Showing the window and ladder exit from *The Book of Bean*.

Model for *The Book of Bean*.

Installation view of
The Book of Bean by
Alison Knowles.

From a Dialogue on Transvironmental Books Between George Quasha and Alison Knowles

A K : The night *The Book of Bean* opened in New York was the night of the blackout in lower New York. Remember? It happened two hours before things were going to begin.

G Q : Synchronistically the whole city became a transvironment.

A K : I came back several times in disbelief. Jess [Alison Knowles' daughter] and I talked to disappointed visitors. A friend of Dan Goode's, a blind saxophonist who was to have performed, was there and asked to be led through the installation. So, we proceeded through the dark, unlighted, unsounded pages. He was delighted with it. He said, "I can see this book with my fingers."

G Q : The roles are reversed. The blind person who is indifferent to the loss of light, reads its texture as the text. He was the only competent reader that night.

A K : With him as a guide I saw things I had not at all considered.

G Q : The artist became the transvironmental reader returned to darkness and incoherence to rediscover the essential book.

A K : And then very dramatically, the lights came on and the tape came up just as we were making our exit. At that point we closed the Book for the night. Another remarkable reader was a dancer named Ramon. I was reading by the soup when he came in one Saturday afternoon to the Franklin Furnace. There was a lot of racket and typing. He took off his shoes and proceeded right into page one, through the tunnel, and passed where I was sitting. Then a voice from upstairs said, "Do you see what that guy is doing?" I looked up to see him climbing the ladder. The typewriters ceased. He walked with perfect balance and arms outstretched toward the center spine. "Please don't touch the page," he murmured. He returned with equal grace. The only person to not just climb the ladder but walk to the middle of the top! I was very impressed and entered him in the roll deck.

GQ: Did you ask him about the experience?

AK: Yes.

• • • •

AK: *The Book of Bean* has a center where things are plugged in, a spine around which the circle turns, and a truck tire inner tube to step through and begin climbing and tunneling through the pages. To help get people into it there are many transparent surfaces to look through and push aside. I notice that I rarely use opaque surfaces. You can always see through something. One is never trapped.

GQ: The idea that you will be surrounded, once inside, is implicit in the transvironmental book. One might get lost in a novel. What we want in a transvironment is to allow this getting lost while supplying a guiding principle that cannot be overly concretized. A book provides a set of perspectives determined by convention: the book in hand, the prayer book or psalter, the view into the world with the head bent slightly forward. When the root metaphor of the book changes, the physiognomy—the posture and attitude— of the reader also changes. The book might be a ceiling, the fresco overhead, the sunroof of the vehicle, an escape-hatch, something you could, if you wished, stick your head through and get a look at an other world. One goes through the Looking Glass or the Mirror in Cocteau's *Orphée*, reversing the flow of life-time. The transfer between book and reader, the transaction, is mediated or translated by a sort of third entity, the conduit of otherness, arising as the genie of reading, the speaker or speakers in the mind's audium, the "impersona" that is always additional to identity. This entity is empty and cannot be defined. It cannot be the object of attention except by a certain intermedial reflection inside the gap.

A K : Your concept of transvironment applies easily to a lot of my work. The first one I made was a hat, a six-foot circle that lowered onto the head from a rope and pulley. It was all transparent paper printed in transparent ink. The sound was made by moving the head and making the cellophane rustle. The colors were backlighted as one looked out, and the visual field was a circle again. It was shown at the hat show on Yam Days.

G Q : That's related to the transvironments I'm building. The simplest model for a transvironment—a dollhouse that one is inside of—is a construction suspended from the ceiling, a "head space" that one gets up under in order to be surrounded by a particular aural and visual field. It contains language, audio and vidio devices, images, non-images, empty spaces, and communication channels disrupting the boundary between inside and outside.

A K : George, couldn't we extend the scale further and have a whole city as the contents of a book? Huge pages as the side of an office building, a single page with water pouring down the front in the park, a page out flat as bridge, as door to the city.

G Q : I've dreamt of such a city all my life, the house or castle with a vast interior. In the transvironmental city one travels to the depths of inside while extending the roads and gardens of outside. It's all one transrupting surface where anything leads to anything else, governed only by imaginal necessities. The book is the instrument by which we tap in on the reading that produced it. We not only could read it, we live in it. Our limbs leave invisible pollen on the pages for the next readers.

Japanese Bean Demon.

Legend has it that a party of Pythagoreans allowed themselves to be slaughtered
by soldiers of Dionysus rather than escape by passing through a bean field.
They have in them the animated matter that is ourselves.

GEORGE QUASHA

Auto-dialogue on the Transvironmental Book:
Reflections on The Book of Bean

What is a transvironment?

Awkwardly stated, a transvironment is a transformationally experienced environment. It is a construct—it may also be a construction or artifact—that creates an opportunity for a fundamental alteration in perception and interpretation of the surrounding world, the context and circumtext. It causes a rupture in plane, a psychotopological catastrophe, a radical transstructuring of texture and text, a literal transfiguration of appearances. It alters the phenomenon of scale, including the relation of self to object (e.g., the book, the window), the function of distance in knowing identity, the comparison of micro- and macro-worlds.

That sounds like art. It is art? If so, is it not all art?

It is art. Art is essentially transvironmental. In fact, life is transvironmental. The environment is always changing, and that keeps us going. But to use so awkward a word as *transvironmental* is to imply a difference of degree that is a difference of kind. Life perceptions in the ordinary are half asleep in their transformations. Art steps up the process. Transvironmental art steps over the edge. The mind goes into freefall and breaks through the membrane of identity. It does this, so to speak, by putting windows in the mirrors and mirrors in the windows.

How does transvironmental art differ from environmental art and installation art?

It may or may not. The term implies a high concentration of context-altering energy within a frame-construct. It not only calls attention in a new way to specific surroundings, as interesting environmental art does; it calls attention as well to the mode and process of attention itself: there is a reflexivity, a rupture of perception onto the plane of conception. And it not only invokes the activity of engaging in the conception, as interesting concept- and installation-art often does; it catastrophizes the concept, floods it with perceptions more radically engaging than the conception, flexes the viewing in its least apparent ocular muscles. It flicks its data at the viewer, causes a blink and, presto, the scene changes.

I see. But how or in what sense is a book transvironmental?

As an object the book is subject to phenomenological qualification. Unlike most other objects it has the power to address its viewer with thoughts, feelings, propositions, images, etc. and in very specific senses it has the power to dialogue with its reader. In this respect it has a range of transvironmental potential that belongs especially to the book. Once it finds its way into your hands or otherwise before your eyes it can play any role. It can tell you what to eat (including, theoretically, itself), thus altering your environment. It can tell you what to think, what to think about *it*, what *not* to think (thus *insuring* that you think it, as in: Do not think of a white horse), what to read other than itself, what to think about the act of reading the text you are reading— and it can at any moment cause a *rupture in the plane of reading*, as, for instance, if you should turn the present page and find the book henceforth blank, or if the ink should begin gradually to fade away, or if the text convinces you that the thoughts you are reading are literally your own and are being plagiarized before your eyes; that the money you paid for the book has gone into the wrong pocket; that the self who lives in your mind has visited this page before you and is now recognizing itself for the first time and you are but its voyeur; that yet other selves who live there and here too are just now coming into view having previously been hidden behind the shadowy image of yourself that blocks the light of past and future alike; that the plane of discourse has been changing bit by bit so that you can no longer be sure of the cognitive routes by which you have reached the present place in the text and therefore you no longer know what to think or what you actually feel; that the text has curiously reserved for itself the right to command you to behave in ways not necessarily appropriate to the book/reader relationship with which you willingly began to read only moments before; that, in short, anything can happen. Imagine that the page you are reading is blank. Relish its blankness. Watch the present words persist even against your best efforts to imagine a blank space here. Stop reading. Now read. Notice that the difficulty experienced in reading such a text may be matched by the difficulty experienced in trying not to read it. Notice the almost palpable presence of your choice to be reading and the obscure boundary of the reading act, the membrane between it and the not-reading that resides on the outside of the book—the outside that may begin with the cover of the book or which may appear at any point within the book itself, where the attention falls off and other thoughts rush in. A book is a kind of Klein bottle: the outsides of the text are linked to the insides of the text via the gaps in attention. Perhaps there is a sentence somewhere in the book which threatens to lead beyond the confines of the book, which takes advantage of the involuntary on-rush of the reading mind hooked on the unfolding story long after any trace of a story has failed to appear, leaving only the words in their stubborn persistence as objects indifferent to a readerly agreement yet strangely capable of invoking ad hoc contexts attractive enough to keep alive the memory of meaning and the hope of eventual edification about who, how, why, when, wherefore, in short, the great questions taking on a personality of their own, speaking to you now as if alive in their own right, emissaries from the great beyond which one hopes is meaningful, strange voices cropping up at random, hauntings and other lacks able to say, for instance: Hello, I am here where you least expect me, I am the voice of   , I am the impersona come to ask a favor of you. Keep reading. Imagine that the words on this page are written in disappearing ink. Imagine that in their place a mirror-like surface is appearing. The words you have written are reading themselves back to you now. They have no other motive but to be here with you. They are hungry for a little late night conversation. They remember you even if you have forgotten them. And yet it is equally true to say of them that this is their first moment of being, that in reading them you give them their only existence, and that therefore they are yours except in the sense that nothing is yours, and that their desire to persist is your desire to continue to be. Their only motive is your fear of death. And their ability to exist here independently of meaning or motive is directly proportionate to your lack of fear of dying. As life energy surges back within you the words become text-degradable and the concepts become mind-degradable. This is an oscillation that is not often experienced directly. Its effect is transvironmental and belongs to the potential of book. Reader reads book and book books reader. If the pattern of this process were projected onto the page in an image of recursive torsion it might describe the figure 8 or, on its side, the sign used for infinity, and the point of self-intersection of the line might be called the event of reflexivity, the catastrophe by which the Klein Book is itself (and not itself), the rupture in the plane of reading where one perceives the text as circum-text or the environment as contained in the frame through which it is seen—the frame that is obviously and inevitably but a small part of the environment. Under no circumstances should you stop reading.

Transactions Between Reader and Text

Life is about taking something from one place and moving it somewhere else. Often the something goes from the outside of something else to the inside of yet another something, or vice versa, such as food, money, germs, genitals, information, etc. Life is a series of transactions to which specific values are given, and culture arises in part from the effort to regularize and assure these transactions. Art plays a paradoxical role, since on the one hand it too attempts to make certain transactions effectively or efficiently happen; yet on the other hand, it attempts to disrupt the more familiar transactional patterns in the interest of reviving or adding to the power of the somethings. The transvironmental is an extreme statement of the latter. It sometimes turns nothings into somethings, or shows the presence of somethings where nothing had appeared. The transvironmental is an enhancement or enlargement of the transactional possiblities, showing that there are more somethings to go more places than was previously known. It does this partly by altering the perceptual organs by which we know any something. A simple texture can become a text which one learns to read. Move some stick around on the beach and it becomes a book. *The Book of Bean* turns beans into signs, notes, conceptual elements, designs. Sperm. It makes the book big enough to encompass or "environ" that which was previously outside the frame of meaning.

List of Possible Transactions Between the Reader and The Book of Bean:

1. Stepping up to begin.

2. Walking through a page.

3. Looking at the pictures.

4. Climbing the ladder to the top.

5. Crawling through a page.

6. Pushing back the curtain.

7. Eating its soup.

8. Listening to the sounds from the time of its making.

9. Focusing on the audible realtime images and sounds.

10. Turning and going in another direction.

11. Leaving it altogether.

12. Turning out the lights.

13. Looking up information in the rolldeck.

14. Stealing a bean and idea from the drawer.

15. Studying books by Beans.

16. Contemplating entering the tunnel.

17. Watching others before and behind.

18. Choosing to read.

19. Choosing not to read.

20. Kneading the beans at the exit.

21. Adding a suggestion to the suggestion box.

22. Sitting down to shoot the breeze.

23. Thinking of additional pages for *The Book of Bean.*

24. Wondering what was meant by burning all that old clothing.

25. Figuring out how the *Book* was made. Would you like to do it?

26. Trying to move the pages.

27. Being distracted.

28. Thinking and talking about the *Book* after you leave it.

29. Trying to get the soup recipe from the artist.

30. Calling people to visit the *Book.*

31. Following somebody else's heart's desire.

Above: Detail from
The Book of Bean.

TINA OLDKNOW

Muslim Soup

FOR SOME TRADITIONAL WEST AFRICAN societies, printed memory in the form of records or books is considered unnatural, even abhorrent. This belief may initially appear strange and foreign to most Western cultures, who place a high priority upon accurate and permanent methods of gathering and recording information. The positive and negative powers of living things, including thoughts, memories and historical events, are understood as embodied in words and, when transferred to written form, are seen as trapped in an undesirable state of rigidity and permanence, a state contrary to life. The recording of negative experiences is considered particularly unhealthy and potentially danergous.

In certain instances, though, the powers harnessed in written words may be perceived as beneficial, and a nonliterate people will sometimes borrow a literate society's script for specific purposes. The Nafana of northwestern Ghana, a nonliterate group familiar with the customs of, and in close contact with, their Muslim neighbors, the Mande, are such an example. Part of the cultural exchange between the Nafana and the Mande is the use of Arabic script by the Nafana, in the form of written charms and verses from the Qur'an. Although the Nafana do not share the Mande's religious beliefs, the power of Islamic magical and holy words is recognized and highly respected. The royal regalia of the Nafana kings commonly have a variety of Muslim amulets attached to them, usually cabalistic signs or Qur'anic verses written on scraps of paper, which are believed to generally protect the objects as well as the king or any other member of the court who might come into contact with them. Important ritual and social areas may also be fortified by the

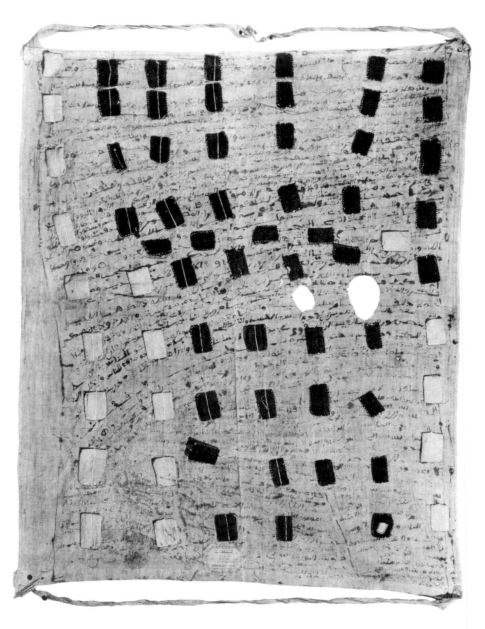

War Dress, Senegal, 10th century, length 39". The Museum of the Philadelphia Civic Center. "The Arabic script and leather amulets were probably meant to make the wearer invulnerable in battle." (From Roy Seiber, *African Textiles and Decorative Arts*, The Museum of Modern Art, NY, 1972.)

placement of similar talismans in strategic spots such as entrances, corners, or other potentially vulnerable boundaries. For especially significant ritual festivities, the king will appear in a special white cloth covered with Arabic letters and signs.

The efficacy of these Islamic charms, adopted by the Nafana from the Mande, extends from the public to the private. As a personal preventative and curative, the power contained in written cabalistic signs and Qur'anic verses may be transformed and condensed into a more potent liquid form, known as *siliama-gue*, or "Muslim soup." This "soup" consists of special roots and herbs steeped in the water used in washing Islamic writing slates or chalkboards. Like the amulets, the tonic made from water used to wash boards with Qur'anic verses on them is believed to be the strongest, the degree of strength determined by the degree of learning attained by the individual writing the verses. As a kind of holy water, "Muslim soup" may be sprinkled onto an individual for protection but is much more effective when drunk. The high success rate of the apotropaic beverage has even been attested to by such claims as invulnerability to gunfire.

The transformation and condensation of the power of Islamic magical and holy writings into liquid form represent, in a sense, the end phase of a cyclic process. If the power of any word may be said to truly lie in its origin in abstract thought, then this power, once translated into literal form, must necessarily be somewhat diminished. From this point of view, the release of a word from a stable, written form to an impermanent, liquid state may be understood as restorative. "Muslim soup" is a method of preparation in which the power of the word is physically freed: it is the word returned to thought.

References

Dennis Duerden, *The Invisible Present: African Art and Literature* (New York, 1975).

René A. Bravmann, *Islamic and Tribal Art in West Africa* (Cambridge, 1974).

A Book

A **BOOK.** Consider a book.

Before one can consider a book, one must consider what it is to have a text. A text is an array of words on paper. Or, if not words, other things that are to be read. One can have a text with no words at all—music or visual entities or symbols.

But when we are talking about art—an art book, the art of language and not just information that is to be used for something other than the experience of being oneself—one must have a self or selves. One need not dwell upon it. But we are all complexes of past experiences and knowledges, each unique unto itself. One need not ask oneself, at the outset, "What is this self? Who is this me that I am being?" One needs no particular ego to experience art. But one does bring a certain horizon to the experience of a book which is its own past and complex of tastes and non-tastes, desires and non-desires, beings and non-beings. Like a ship moving towards a horizon, that horizon always recedes, no matter in what direction one moves. The complex of what one knows and what one does not know and what one knows without consciously considering it, that horizon is always in motion. And the text that is a work of art brings its horizon to us. The horizons intersect and interpenetrate.

Authors make texts when they offer us arrays of words which generate horizons that interpenetrate with ours, when they displace ours in the course of this interpenetration. The author is supremely unimportant while we are studying a text. If we want to know about apples, if we want to study why apples are as they are, *then* we must study about appletrees. But when we are hungry, we do not study about apples. We eat them. So it is with texts and authors. When we are hungry to experience our horizons in motion, the author is beside the point; here it is the text which that author has made that is important. For us it is our experience of the text which we are living with, not the text which the author thought he made. When Samuel Richardson wrote *Clarissa* he thought that he was making a series of morally exemplary letters—prudish, perhaps. Instead he created what we experience as one of the most erotic novels in our language, erotic in its curious horizon of dwelling forever upon sexual innuendo. Lately most criticism has dwelt upon the linguistics of the text, upon the structure and *langue* and *parole* and semiotics of the work. But judged as experience, that is relatively unimportant, since it is the effect of the style which is so crucial, the phenomenon of the generation of the horizons of Clarissa and her circle and how they fit and do not fit with ours. Same with Gertrude Stein, whose focus is upon the language of her horizon and ours: it is displacement. A structuralist and a semiotician would go mad trying to explain why Stein works when "it" (her work) works. For us, enjoying the displacements of our horizons of language by hers, there is no problem. We each have our own horizons, our own hermeneutic for this (our own methodology of interpretation). I can document mine, and each human being who reads a Stein can learn to document hers or his. But the gut feelings that the work generates, the emotional and connotative and phatic elements, these do not come from what she says but from the process of matching how she says it with our own horizons.

A text can be spread over space without becoming a book. We can write it on a scroll and experience it as never-ending, unbroken. Most texts seem to have been written for experience upon scrolls—perhaps their authors think of life as scrolls. In point of fact, of course, scrolls have their own interesting qualities, their physicality and their unique continuity.

But a book, in its purest form, is a phenomenon of space and time and dimensionality that is unique unto itself. Every time we turn the page, the previous page passes into our past and we are confronted by a new world. In my *Of Celebration of Morning*, my book qua book which uses these ideas most purely, I even called each page "world 1," "world 2," and so on through the eighty pages. The only time a text exists in a solid block of time is when we are no longer reading it, unlike, for example, a single painting which is all present before us when we consider its presence physically. In this way a book is like music, which is only experienced moment by moment until it, too, is past and remembered as a whole. But the space of the book, even when it is not self-consciously shaped and patterned (as in visual novels or concrete poetry or comic books), is part of the experience. *Alice in Wonderland* written out by hand is a different work from *Alice in Wonderland* set in type; set in Baskerville, even, it is a different entity from what it would become set in some barely-legible but beautiful Old English blackletter face. It is, as it were, translated when it is set from one face to another, just as surely as if it had been paraphrased into another language. All literature exists only in translation for this reason—it is displaced from the author's intention, displaced visually by being presented to us upon the page, displaced by us conceptually every time we experience it by reading it, displaced according to our horizons at the moment. One time we read a text with passion, one time coolly, one time in a desultory way, one time with great attention to the characters and gestalts generated by the text, another time with our eye on the horizons of our language and that of the text.

The book is, then, the container of provocation. We open it and are provoked to match our horizons with those implied by the text. We need not consider ourselves to do this; but the more vivid our horizons and the more vivid the gestalts and horizons in the text, the more vivid the displacements and coincidences of these horizons. And therein lies the true pleasure of the text, the true erotic of literature. Criticism which ignores this does so at its peril—it may be fashionable for a moment but it will die. Great criticism always keeps its eye on the horizons of the work at hand and so, like Coleridge's lectures on Shakespeare, always exists upon three horizons of time—its subject's, the critic's and ours. Perhaps that is the crucial difference between criticism and poetry, for example—the first has three horizons, the latter has two to offer. Not that "the more the merrier," of course. Two horizons can be plenty.

But the book that is clear upon what horizons it can offer up for our experience (whatever nonsense its author may have intended it to be), that book is well upon its way to matching its horizons with ours and is, thus, on the track of potential greatness.

There is no need to bother with the rest.

DAVID MELTZER

From the Rabbi's Dream Book

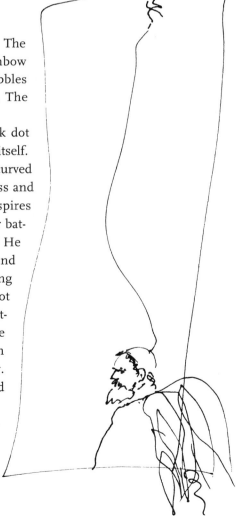

AT THE END OF A SENTENCE. The dot. A stop. A blank circle. Its edges rainbow like petroleum like linoleum like bubbles blown out of plastic hoops. The period. The end. A stop.

Black round sphere on the page. Black dot holding all the alphabets and words inside itself.

Did you ever see the angel who wears a curved and no doubt jewel-powered device of glass and metals looped about into mad-scientist spires and gyres and all of it hooked to transistor batteries worn around his arms like snakes? He puts his mouth on a tuba mouthpiece and blows four notes which you can see moving up the tubing, turning into one black dot rushing up through loops and hoops of metals and glass. The black dot goes up to the top shaped like an upside-down icecream brass cone and out it goes. Into the air. Straight to the ope n book's blank page and it lands right in the white center.

Black dot in the center of a page surrounded by white. The period. The end. A stop.

Another angel who wasn't in the room before appears through the roof in a flurry of splashing light like overflowing fireworks. And lands before the large open book and shuts his eyes and slowly lets his wings fold together. Light remaining from his flight falls onto the floor where it dissolves like snowflakes.

—I am the Angel of the Alphabet, he says to the open book.

The book says nothing.

But the black dot widens in the page's center and opens like a yawn like an apple sliced into many sudden wedges. And the Angel of the Alphabet seems pleased and flutters his wings like a helicopter and arises to the ceiling and soaks through it like sunlight.

Period. The end. A stop. The room is empty again. Its walls as white as blank pages in the book. There is nothing in the room. Period. Except the book which is on a round table made from sturdy wood and engraved and carved with stars, moons, alphabets, hieroglyphs, petroglyphs, runes going around the edges of the table.

Letter into letter into letter. The black dot splinters into black shapes of lovely designs. Flowers quickly blossoming. People walking. Each letter as it forms itself looks like something remembered from life. An ox, a coathook, a dancer, a room, a staff, a pitchfork, a stem, a seed, a weed.

Letters appear on the page and meet each other to form words. They stand in groups and sing. They discuss each other's meanings. They remember and they forget.

A black angel spreads its black wings through a wall of the rooms and enters. He is happy to see the page of the books alive with his blackness. His shadow is like a letter on a white wall.

A white angel, entirely white, spreads its wings and enters through the wall as if breaking through water after diving deep into a lake and then pushing up and up to where sunlight wobbles and shatters on the water.

The two angels stand side by side before the book. Their black and white shadows.

And we know that the black angel shuts his eyes as if asleep and all the letters and words float to him and he inhales them as if smelling a stew. And we know he turns an eye-blinking white from head to toe, dazzling.

And we know how the white angel smiles to see the book page suddenly empty of marks. And we are ready when he shuts his eyes and the pages of the book turn faster than a cartoon and become a small snowstorm which the white angel inhales and, to our amazement, turns a magnificent black.

And later, when the sun and moon and stars have turned inside out into letters and pages and words and books, and a century of amazing seconds has gone, and it's hard to know what's happening, but nobody's worried, a comforting voice says to you or me or to nobody in particular that the black dot is the planet of the alphabet. The alphabet atom. All alphabets live in harmony in the period. The stop. The end.

And the blank page, white and empty, is the alphabet's sky.

And sometimes what has been said seems to be true. The letters and words are stars in the white sky of the page. Or the white page is part of a huge letter with dots and spots of black sky poking through it.

And now what do you say if we start all over again?

At the end of the sentence. Dot. Stop. Black circle. Beginning again.

Notes on
Codex Vienna

WE KNOW THAT BOOK PRODUCTION flourished in pre-Conquest Mexico. Among the types of books produced were genealogies, histories, books for interpreting dreams and determining suitable marriage partners, law books, bureaucratic documents and a wide range of religious books. At least three formats were simultaneously in use: the screenfold, the scroll, and the *lienzo* (a large piece of cloth that could be folded up like a sheet)— and several other forms are hinted at. Unfortunately, only about a dozen pre-Conquest books have survived from central Mexico, though we also have a number of post-Conquest books produced more or less in the indigenous style. *Codex Vienna* is one of the pre-Conquest books that has survived.

This manuscript is painted on 15 strips of deerskin, glued together to form a single band about 44'3" long and about 9" tall. It is folded accordion fashion so that there are 52 pages on each side, each about 10-3/4" across. The ends are glued onto wooden boards, leaving only 50 pages open for painting on the reverse side. All 52 pages of the front are painted, while the painting breaks off in the middle of the thirteenth page of the reverse. Chemical analysis has not been made of the manuscript, but we may assume that it was painted with the same materials as other books of its type: a ground of lime gesso was first applied to the entire surface, lines were drawn using a carbon-base ink, and color was filled in afterward, using the basic pigments—mineral blue, yellow and red oxide, and possibly cochineal base red; other colors, used sparingly, were probably combinations of the basic pigments. Though we can't be sure at this point what kind of applicators were used, two instruments that may be a pen and a brush are shown at the middle right of page

35 (18) in the *Codex*. Most scholars agree that this book was produced in the Mixtec area to the south of Mexico City.

The first side of the manuscript tells of the creation of the world and the Mixtec people. It lists the places within the Mixtec area and defines its lordships. It relates the struggles and interactions of the Mixtecs with the Stonemen—possibly Teotihuacan colonizers or Toltec conquerors—and the history of their most important plants: corn, maguey, and hallucinogenic mushrooms. After the prologue dealing with the creation of the world and the Mixteca, the book is divided into ten major chapters, each centering on the New Fire ceremony that began historic and mythic eras, and showing related rituals in minute detail. The main personage in the book is the form of the god Quetzalcoatl known as 9-Wind, after the date of his birth. This god plays a crucial role in the creation of the world and the establishment of the Mixtec lordships, and it is he who lights New Fire for the first time. The book tells the story of the Mixteca in a general, mythic, almost extrahistorical sense. It is one of the most beautiful examples of pre-Columbian bookmaking we have. It seems to be the product of a serene and unhurried workshop, whose artists had received long and rigorous training in both the techniques of book manufacture and in the religion and history of their people.

The reverse side is a reverse indeed: it is probably the worst example of indigenous painting we have. Its creator does not seem to have been particularly skilled but he does seem to have been working at breakneck speed. Toward the end, he simply lists names, without accompanying images. This side of the manuscript records the lineage of the House of Tilontongo from A.D. 720 to the middle of the 14th century. We may conjecture that side I was painted at royal command during a relatively stable period of Mixtec history. Side 2 was then added when that stability was broken by an invasion from one of the city-states around Lake Texcoco, perhaps Colhuacan. The vanquished Mixtecs may have sent the book as tribute to their conquerors, after someone had hastily painted the lineage of their house on the back as evidence of their legitimate claim to their lands.

In his *Prymera Relación* of 1519, Cortez wrote that he was sending "two books such as the Indians use" along with other loot to Charles V of Spain.

We can feel fairly certain that *Codex Vienna* was one of them because an ownership inscription on the manuscript says that Charles V gave it to Manuel I of Portugal who was dead by the time the next consignment of Mexican plunder reached Europe. Cortez probably obtained the book in one of two ways. Since the recto of the manuscript centers on Quetzalcoatl, and since Moctezoma believed that Cortez was either a manifestation or a lieutenant of that god, he may have sent it to the Spaniard with other gifts shortly after Cortez landed on the Mexican coast. We have record of a consignment of gifts sent by Moctezoma along with the message that Mexico was still being well managed, that its people still venerated Quetzalcoatl, and that there was no need for the god to come to the capital. This book would certainly have been an appropriate one to send with such a collection of gifts, since it would seem to confirm Moctezoma's message. The other possibility also involves Quetzalcoatl's prominence in the book. Before the invasion began, Moctezoma had disaffected large segments of the indigenous nobility by reducing their privileges and meddling in affairs they considered their own. One of his major activities during this period seems to have been seeking omens about the return of Quetzalcoatl and then trying to circumvent or hide from them. One of his approaches to the problem was to systematically gather books that dealt with the god, have them searched for omens, and then destroyed if the omens were unfavorable. Moctezoma had heard that one such book was in the hands of two lords, Atonal and Tlamapanatzin, and he ordered them to burn the book. These lords were among those disaffected by Moctezoma. They thought that such a book would help anyone wishing to overthrow the emperor and secretly approached Cortez, who was then on the coast, offering him the book and their support if he would unseat Moctezoma and restore them to their former status. Cortez, of course, accepted the offer. He probably couldn't think of anything to do with the book except send it back to Spain with his first consignment of exotic loot, but it was the sort of aid that these two lords offered that gave him key advantages over Moctezoma and made the rapid conquest of Mexico possible.

We can reconstruct part of the book's history in Europe. Between the time Cortez received it and the time at which it came to the Austrian National

Library, where it now resides, it was owned by two emperors, a king, a duke, a pope, and three cardinals—the list includes two Medicis and a Hapsburg. Clearly, during the first 350 years of its European career, it functioned as a pawn in the game of political flattery, a token to curry favor. Thus the book took part in at least two major conquests in Mexico and, in a quiet way, hovered behind its share of aristocratic intrigue in Europe.

Little has been written to date on how indigenous books were used, even though, as far as I can tell, they don't make much sense outside the context of their use. When their use has been considered, it has usually been asserted that they were simply mnemonic devices—that their images reminded readers of things they would not otherwise remember. This may have been the case with bureaucratic documents like the *Matriculo de Tributos,* but makes no sense at all for a manuscript like the obverse of *Codex Vienna.* Moreover, the indigenous Mexicans, being in our sense preliterate, probably didn't need devices to remind them of their history and mythology: their memories were probably excellent and they probably had several orders of professional singers of myths, histories, genealogies, etc., not unlike the Yugoslavian "Singers of Tales" described by Lord and Parry, and the West African "Singers of Genealogies" brought to popular attention in this country by *Roots.* Space does not allow a thorough discussion of reading methods in pre-Conquest Mexico, but I will suggest several uses to which this manuscript could have been put.

The first I'll mention was probably the most important, and it is partly mnemonic, *but* it approaches memory from the other end. We have a fairly large body of information—including numerous citations from Sahagún's informants—which indicates that painted books and recitation of verse were major parts of education. As teaching tools the books were probably used to engrave myth and history, in a form that could be internally visualized, in the minds of students—in other words, their purpose was not to remind people of things they might otherwise forget, but to make those things unforgettable. The brilliant and simple colors, the decisive black frameline, the crystalline clarity of images, and the vibrant paratactic compositions—the basic qualities of indigenous style—are perfectly suited to this purpose. Students would imbed innumerable myths, histories, genealogies, prayers, etc., in verse form in their minds along with the visual images. The words and images need not have explained or commented on one another—each may have balanced, complemented, or extended the other, and each probably gave the student something the other couldn't. The visual and aural components of their education would then inform their dreams, their visions, their notions of the world, and their actions throughout their lives.

A number of sources tell us that books of this sort were mounted, fully extended, on walls on certain occasions. We may assume that these occasions were of a ritual nature and that the books served a ritual rather than a decorative function. We can imagine readers standing before the mounted books, reciting the verses they'd learned in youth, as they visually reaffirmed and refurbished the images in their minds. A number of people acting in this manner would somewhat resemble contemporary participants in a performance, say, of Jackson Mac Low's *Gathas*—performers achieving a high degree of concentration on the images before them and on the sounds they utter, and simultaneously feeling a sense of community with the other performers. We shouldn't, however, push this parallel too far: a contemporary performance would not involve the same stored energy and association as did those of pre-Conquest Mexico, but would include a sense of exploration not present in the older type of performance.

Books of a historical nature may have been used in the singing of epics. In this type of situation, a small audience would sit around the singer, who would place the book between himself and his audience, unfolding it as he sang. In this case, the book would act not so much as a score for the singer as it would a visual counterpart to the song, for the audience to contemplate as they listened. Books could also be read privately by adults. In such instances, we should not assume that a private reading was a silent reading, as it usually is with us; private readers probably recited verses of all sorts as they read. For adults, the books probably did not convey new information, but rather deepened what the readers already knew. With some of the religious books, this kind of reading may have been an important part of an internal self-discipline, not unlike the Oriental practices we call yoga. Certainly many of the religious books could have been used in visualization exercises like those practiced by Tibetan Buddhists, and this may have been an important stage in the deity impersonation that was so important to indigenous Mexican religion. The central section of *Codex Borgia* may even be considered as a set of mandalas. The religious books, containing lists, charts, and calendars used in divination and in organizing rituals, would be read in a different manner than less compartmentalized books. The reader may only have been looking for a date in a calendar, but he probably did so in a prescribed manner, reciting verses as he proceeded.

The screenfold format is well suited to these different types of reading. The "Singer of Epics" could spread out as many pages as necessary before his audience. The whole book could be mounted on a wall in ceremonial situations. When held in a reader's hands, a book of this type can be organized in different ways by folding up pages and creating juxtapositions of pages. For instance, if a reader wished to juxtapose page 1 and page 6 of a book, he could simply fold the intervening pages together, placing I and 6 next to each other. This would be particularly useful in using ritual-calendrical books, where charts, diagrams, and calendars would be compared and correlated. In histories it could also have been useful. The indigenous Mexicans had a cyclical conception of history, and this format would allow comparison of one cycle with another. In *Codex Vienna,* it would allow comparison and collateral reading of any 2 of the book's 11 parts (prologue and 10 chapters), each of which is centered on the lighting of new fire and hence on a period of mythic time. The lists of places—each of which seems to approach the Mixteca from a different perspective—could be interrelated in this format: places as geographic entities could be aligned with political lordships. And, of course, all other parts of the book could be used in conjunction with the ritual sections.

An interesting feature of pre-Conquest books is that they can be given what I call a brief or an extended reading. In a brief reading, the reader simply identifies the figures in the book and their functions. An extensive reading would involve a great deal more: the reader would recite large portions of the verse associated with each image, though not necessarily contained in it. Let's say the page begins with the figure of a god: the reader begins with a lengthy invocation of the god, lists his powers and attributes, narrates his most relevant myths, and perhaps ends with a prayer. The next figure is a man: the reader recites his genealogy, his biography, maxims associated with him, and so forth. A brief reading of a page could take several minutes; an extended reading, several hours. I don't think we can hope to re-create an extensive reading of any of the pages of *Codex Vienna*, but a brief reading seems possible, and that is what I have attempted in the "translation" of the three pages presented here. Of course, since our knowledge of the books and the world they functioned in is limited, and since nearly everything we do know is interpreted differently by different contemporary students of these books, such a reading must be considered tentative.

A few brief notes on indigenous conventions should be made before presenting my "translations." Most pre-Conquest deities existed in numerous and often bewildering variant forms. In this manuscript, a number of distinct forms of the god Quetzalcoatl are presented, but the one distinguished by the calendar name 9-Wind is the most important. Dates were written by a combination of one of the twenty day-signs and a numeral from 1 to 13, indicated by the appropriate number of dots. 9-Wind is represented by a wind-mask and nine dots. Each day in the indigenous calendar had a specific fate and the pre-Conquest Mexicans and their gods took their birth dates as their names, since the date defined who they were. Hence 9-Wind is both the name of a specific manifestation of Quetzalcoatl and the date of birth of that manifestation. In some of the historical manuscripts, like *Bodley* and *Selden*, dates not used as names are simply dates, little different in function from our December 3 or August 12. In *Codex Vienna*, however, dates not used as names of persons or gods probably have a mythic rather than a chronological significance. This book is not a history in our sense of the word: an event takes place on a specific date because that's the date in the indigenous calendar on which such an event has the most significance.

I use the Nahuatl names of deities here. The people who first used this book probably had different, Mixtec names for them, but they are unknown to us at the present time. A problem that remains unsolved is to what extent the Mixtec notions of these deities varied from those of the peoples of the

Valley of Mexico, where we have more extensive documentation in European script (and hence names of the deities). We do, however, use the name Buddha when discussing Indian, Chinese, Japanese, Tibetan, and Burmese religion, even though this figure (and his name) varies from one context to the next. I think we can do the same here, provided that we bear in mind the possibility of significant local variation.

Reading begins in the lower right hand corner of each page. Start there and follow the arrows in my translation. Generally, reading proceeds in boustrophedon or meander pattern. There is an exception to this rule on page 5: when you come to the bottom of the second column, you do not proceed up the third, but rather start over again at the top of column three. The painter of the manuscript probably interrupted the normal pattern of reading here to emphasize the important event depicted in this column.

As part of my study of this manuscript, I have painted a facsimile of it. I recommend this sort of activity to any serious student of these manuscripts. It provides insights that I don't think could be gained by simply looking at a facsimile, and perhaps, in a small way, helps to make up for the loss of the oral counterpart of the book—at least it allows the reader to participate on an active level. The reproductions used here are from my painted copy.

Codex Vienna, page 1.

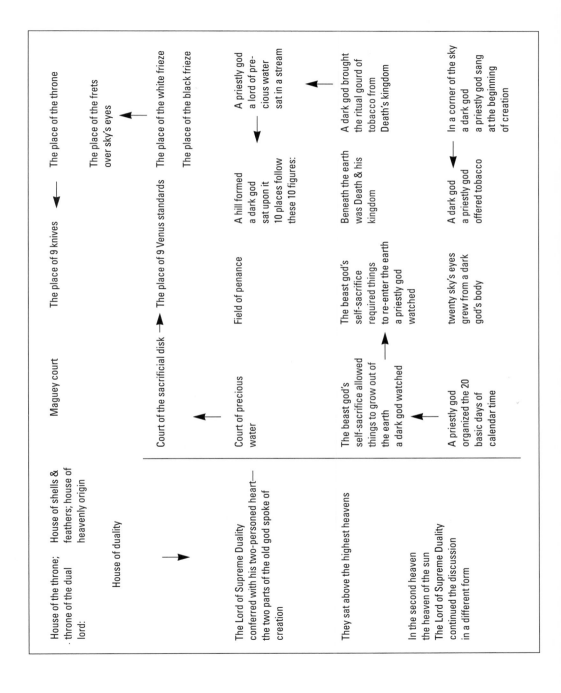

House of the throne;
throne of the dual
lord:

House of shells &
feathers; house of
heavenly origin

House of duality

The place of the throne

The place of the frets
over sky's eyes

The place of 9 knives

The place of 9 Venus standards

The place of the white frieze

The place of the black frieze

Maguey court

Court of the sacrificial disk

Court of precious
water

Field of penance

A hill formed
a dark god
sat upon it
10 places follow
these 10 figures:

A priestly god
a lord of pre-
cious water
sat in a stream

The Lord of Supreme Duality
conferred with his two-personed heart—
the two parts of the old god spoke of
creation

The beast god's
self-sacrifice allowed
things to grow out of
the earth
a dark god watched

The beast god's
self-sacrifice
required things
to re-enter the earth
a priestly god
watched

Beneath the earth
was Death & his
kingdom

A dark god brought
the ritual gourd of
tobacco from
Death's kingdom

They sat above the highest heavens

A priestly god
organized the 20
basic days of
calendar time

twenty sky's eyes
grew from a dark
god's body

A dark god
a priestly god
offered tobacco

In a corner of the sky
a dark god
a priestly god sang
at the beginning
of creation

In the second heaven
the heaven of the sun
The Lord of Supreme Duality
continued the discussion
in a different form

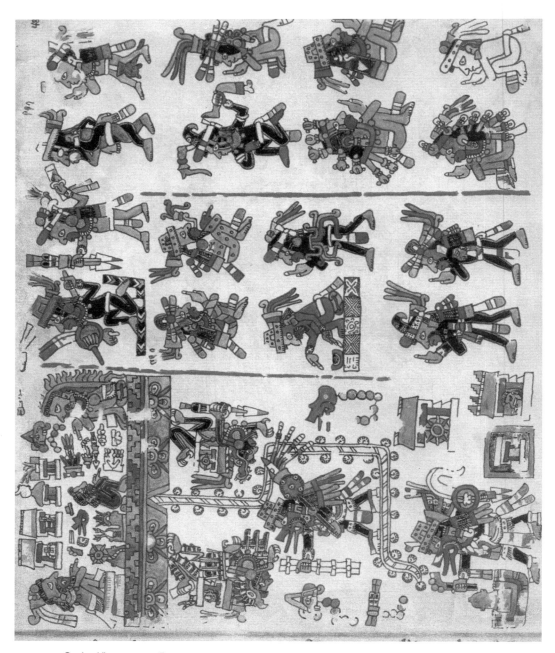

Codex Vienna, page 5.

Old Councilor God

The dark & naked god, not yet empowered, sat in the divine presence, below the temples of Quetzalcoatl, surrounded by his attributes

Lord of Supreme Duality

In the Year 6-Rabbit, on the Day 7-Reed, the gods agreed to invest 9-Wind Quetzalcoatl with his attributes & powers

An eagle-man angel, carrying the temple of sacrifice descended with him

A turtle fire-snake angel, carrying the sun's temple descended with him

the sky opened:

on a rope of shells & feathers,

in the Year 6-Rabbit, Day 5-Reed,

he descended, carrying the Venus staff & Earth sceptre, the symbols of his office

he landed as a warrior, with darts, shield, & obsidian sword; he first took possession of these places:

Temple of the Sun
Temple of Sacrifice
Temple of Darkness

Primal Island

A dark god, a patron of warriors, brought his powers to the council; kneeling on a warpath, he prepared for the coming of 9-Wind Quetzalcoatl

A twisted god, a patron of artificers, brought his powers to the council; he prepared for the coming of 9-Wind Quetzalcoatl

A light god, with a censer, a director of ritual, a guide for offerings, brought his powers to the council; he prepared for the coming of 9-Wind Quetzalcoatl

A light god, a patron of warriors, carrying darts & a spear-thrower, brought his powers to the council; he prepared for the coming of 9-Wind Quetzalcoatl

A god with a jaguar's body, a patron of warriors, carrying darts & a spearthrower, brought his powers to the council; he prepared for the coming of 9-Wind Quetzalcoatl

A dark god, wearing the knife of twisted obsidian at his head, a patron of sacrifice & penance, brought his powers to the council; kneeling in the warrior's posture, holding an enemy's leg, he prepared for the coming of 9-Wind Quetzalcoatl

A light god, with windblades in the curled hair of the death gods, a lord of generation, brought his powers to the council; he prepared for the coming of 9-Wind Quetzalcoatl

A god made of stone, a god of instruction, a patron of teachers, with windblades at his head, brought his powers to the council; he prepared for the coming of a 9-Wind Quetzalcoatl

A red god, a lord of the east, a painter of sacred books, brought his powers to the council; seated over a book of the central constellations of the sky, pointing to the ashes from which man would be made, he prepared for the coming of 9-Wind Quetzalcoatl

A dark god, a patron of mystics, with the generative song of sacrifice coming from his heart brought his powers to the council; he prepared for the coming of 9-Wind Quetzalcoatl

A solar god, with 9 gold bells, a patron of workers in precious metal, brought his powers to the council; he prepared for the coming of 9-Wind Quetzalcoatl

A bearded god, wearing the wind's headdress, a lord of wind, a lord of omens, brought his powers to the council; he prepared for the coming of 9-Wind Quetzalcoatl

A dark god, wearing the knife bundle of twisted obsidian, a god of sacrifice & penance, he prepared for the coming of 9-Wind Quetzalcoatl

A dark god, with the image of Xolotl's sacrifice deep in his heart, brought his powers to the council; he prepared for the coming of 9-Wind Quetzalcoatl

A blue god, a god of jade, a god of rain & penance, a lord of the west, brought his powers to the council; he prepared for the coming of 9-Wind Quetzalcoatl

A white god, a patron of cotton & snow, brought his powers to the council; he prepared for the coming of 9-Wind Quetzalcoatl

These 16 gods, these 8 pairs, were other forms of the god Quetzalcoatl

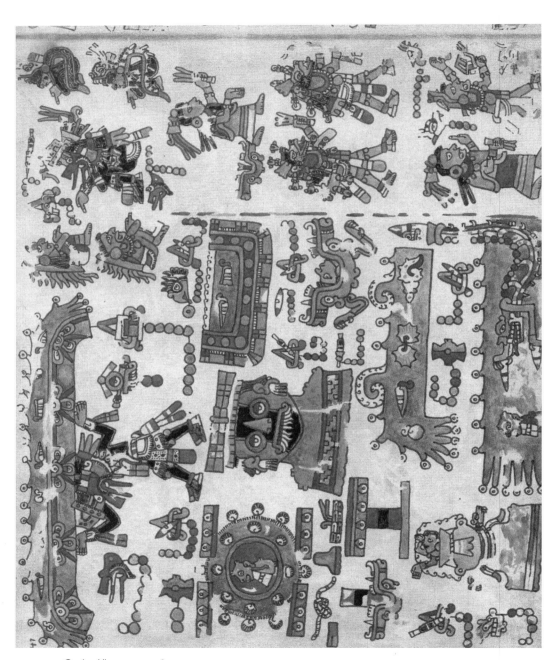

Codex Vienna, page 6.

In the Year 10-House, on the Day 2-Rain, 9-Wind Quetzalcoatl separated the celestial waters from the waters of Earth & waters of Death; he raised the waters that would become rain into his shoulders & fixed them in the sky

The two-personed

Ocelot Snake, a son of the Supreme Duality

Jaguar Snake, a son of the Supreme Duality

9-Wind Quetzalcoatl

Lord of Duality

Held a conference in the year 5-Rabbit, day 5-Reed, giving 9-Wind Quetzalcoatl dominion over the waters

An earth goddess offered penitential grass on earth's behalf

The blue Xolotl, patron of rain, wearing jade pendants, like falling drops of water, offered penitential rods

Year 7-Reed, day 7-Reed, day of origins, Mount Tlaloc was founded, & given dominion over rain

Year 10-Flint, Day 1-Eagle, 9-Wind Quetzalcoatl reserved the most precious waters, some to be sacred lakes under the regency of Our Lady Precious Jade Skirt, some to be hidden away in sacred mountains, ruled by Tepeyolotli, the heart of the mountain, some to be stored in men for use in battle and in sacrifice

The gold Xolotl, patron of lightning, wearing thunder bells, offered penitential grass

Year 5-Flint, Day 5-Flint, 9-Wind Quetzalcoatl founded the caves in the earth from which men would take their origin

4-Dog, the old creator goddess, offered penitential grass, and spoke her mind

8-Alligator, the old creator god, offered tobacco, a wreath, & a bird

Year 8-Flint, Day 2-Movement, Xolotl, Quetzalcoatl's twin, the god whose sacrifice allowed heavenly bodies to rise and set, was placed in the center of the sky, in a hoop of stars and feathers, and charged with the regulation of day and night and with the change of seasons

In the Year 5-Flint, Day 8-Movement, 9-Wind Quetzalcoatl separated the terrestrial waters and the River of Generations (from which the Mixtecs come) from the waters of Death's Kingdom Xolotl passed through the Rivers of Death

Year 5-Reed, Day 7-Grass, 9-Wind Quetzalcoatl recalled Xolotl's sacrifice and the mortifications he would have to endure in the ongoing process of creation

Major Sources Used

Codex Vindobonensis I—color facsimile, ed. & with brief notes by Otto Adelhofer. Akademische Druck. Verlagsanstalt, Graz, Austria, 1963.

C.A. Burland, "More on Codex Vindobonensis Mexicanus I." *Katunob*, #5, Colorado State College, Greeley, 1966.

Alfonso Caso, "Explicación del Reverso del Codex Vindobonensis." *Memoria del Colegio Nacional*, vol. 5, #5, Mexico City, 1951.

Alfonso Caso, "Representaciones de Hongos en los Códices." *Estudios de Cultura Nahuatl*, #4, Mexico City, 1963.

José Corona Núñez, "Explicación del Códice Vindobonensis." *Antigüedades de México*, vol. 4, Secretaria de Hacienda y Crédito Público, Mexico City, 1967.

Francisco López de Gomara, *Cortés*, trans. Lesley Byrd Simpson. University of California Press, Los Angeles, 1964.

Karl Anton Nowotny, *Tlacuilolli*. lbero-Amerikanische Bibliotek, *Monumenta Americana*, 3, Berlin, 1961.

Donald Robertson, *Mexican Manuscript Painting of the Early Colonial Period*. Yale University Press, New Haven, 1961.

Fray Bernardino de Sahagún, *The Florentine Codex*, C. Dibble & J. O. Anderson, eds. & trans. School of American Research, Santa Fe & University of Utah, eleven vols., 1950-1969.

Mary Elizabeth Smith, *Picture Writing from Ancient Southern Mexico: Mixtec Place Signs and Maps*. University of Oklahoma Press, Norman, 1973.

Suggestions for Further Reading

The Akademische Druck facsimiles of Meso-American pictorial manuscripts (distributed in the U.S. by the Current Co.) are generally considered the best available at the present time—but they are expensive: their edition of *Vienna* (which they call *Vindobonensis*, the Latin name of the bookused in older sources) currently bears the retail price of $385.40. If you have access to a good academic library, you might want to check their special collections department for copies of these facsimiles. You might also check for the Sociedad Mexicana de Antropología facsimiles of codices *Bodley, Colombino, and Selden,* which were published along with superb commentaries by Alfonso Caso. The only inexpensive facsimile of a central Mexican pre-Conquest manuscript currently available is the Dover edition of *Codex Nuttall* ($7.95, paper). This book, which has an excellent introduction by Arthur G. Miller, is actually a facsimile of a turn-of-the-century facsimile. Given the limitations of turn-of-the-century stone lithography, this is an excellent facsimile—but it pales in comparison to the Akademische Druck editions. Compare the details reproduced in John Paddock's *Ancient Oaxaca* (Stanford University Press, 1966) with the corresponding passages in the Dover edition. Paddock's book, by the way, includes a color reproduction of page 1 of *Vienna,* and can give you a sense of how the first of the three pages presented here looks in color, if none of the complete color facsimiles is available to you. The initial chapters of Smith's *Picture Writing* provide a good introductory summary of conventions used in the pictorial manuscripts (the rest is a detailed study of place signs and maps). There are brief comments on several pages of *Vienna* in the relatively easy to find *Image of the New World* by Gordon Brotherston (Thames & Hudson, 1979) and *The Wondrous Mushroom* by R. Gordon Wasson (McGraw, 1980). J. Eric S. Thompson's *A Commentary on the Dresden Codex* (American Philosophical Society, 1972) provides a relatively inexpensive ($35) facsimile + important commentary on a pre-Conquest book from the Mayan area. A good place to start studying the pictorial manuscripts is provided by the two comprehensive bibliographies, Ignacio Bernal's *Bibliografía de Arqueología y Etnografía* and Howard F. Cline's *Guides to Ethnohistorical Sources,* volumes 14 & 15 of *Handbook of Middle American Indians.*

EDMOND JABÈS

The Book and the Desert/[Wilderness]:
An Interview

LIBÉRATION: At first glance, one has the impression that these books, all interconnected in the two series, *The Book of Questions* and *The Book of Resemblances*, come from far away, not only geographically but with respect to language and history as well…then how did it begin?

E. JABÈS: Through a break. These books were not premeditated. They imposed themselves on me after my break with Egypt, where I was born. In 1957 I was obliged to leave that country without knowing very well to what extent it was an integral part of me. It was difficult for me to tally it up to myself accurately. With French education—I was naturalized in 1967—my eyes were turned toward France. And then, down there, I was above all a product of my social condition, my trade, which had nothing to do with literature.

The fact that I write was something extra. I suffered as well from being considered a sort of amateur, whereas I felt myself already completely integral with French literature, close to many of its writers. I recognized myself in a thread that you can find in my poems, *I Build My Dwelling*: I was very early influenced by Baudelaire and Rimbaud. Then my meeting with Max Jacob was a crucial one.

Finally there were also the Surrealists. All those poets were my family. On arriving in France I thought I would be able to integrate myself into that literary family but on the contrary a schism occurred. This is even more paradoxical considering that *I Build My Dwelling*, appearing in 1959, two years after I'd come to Paris, was so well received by my friends, writers I respected and who accepted me entirely. It was curiously enough at that moment that I felt myself most detached from that literary connection you would have thought had profoundly entered me.

I found myself in total darkness. Only my wife and I were conscious of what was happening. I began to write *The Book of Questions*, which helped to sustain me outside of literature. I spoke to no one of this uneasiness. Not even to Gabriel Bounoure, who very quickly realized it—nor to other, close friends. I was more than ever riveted on the French language, my only language, but through a book that surpassed me and that looked like no book you'd have expected from me.

I must add that what I believe is subversive in my works, which you yourself have emphasized more than once, is expressed in a writing that is perfectly classical. You can't always tell what's subversive in these books, what's behind the words; but they are clearly written. No phrase isn't worked over. I've explained myself elsewhere in this way.

LIBÉRATION: I'd like to return to that fundamental break which finally gave birth to the whole of your work. A break with Egypt, but more precisely, why? What did Egypt represent to you at that time? What kind of place? Or non-place?

E. JABÈS: Yes, why? It's important. I left Egypt because I was a Jew. I had only a distant rapport with Judaism. Even so, I never denied the fact that I was a Jew. But in Egypt at that time you didn't have to explain yourself in terms of your origins. They accepted you as you were. There were French, English, Italians and among them French Jews, English Jews, Italian Jews. I never experienced anti-Semitism in Egypt except for the last years, when life became intolerable for Jews.

So, leaving Egypt because I was a Jew, I found myself confronted with my Jewish condition, a little in spite of myself, because of my condition as an exile. And that place, that non-place which you speak of, which at the same time is the place of all my books, is the desert. The experience of the desert that I had in Egypt and that my writings only took possession of after the break with that land, was a determining factor for me. The desert forces you to strip yourself of everything extra.

The stripping by the desert is difficult to take on, it's close to death.

It was only after arriving in France that I began to relive that experience, from the inside. From this was born an entire questioning along the line of a memory more ancient than remembrances. And some stories. In particular the story of the camps. I had never been in the camps but I evidently experienced that insupportable injustice, that evil, in the depths of my being, as a Jew and as a man.

So it is around a story that *The Book of Questions* begins: an imaginary and at the same time banal account, banal because of the repetition of the drama, because of the camps. It concerns a young deported couple, Sarah and Yukel, adolescents who love each other. When Sarah returns to France she's lost her mind and Yukel ends up killing himself. The cries of the madness of Sarah then come forth mingling with the millennial lament, the millennial cry of an oppressed collectivity. These are therefore symbols.

And taking off from there, a whole reflection, not merely an intellectual one, was developed. The question was: What does the word culture mean, after Auschwitz? What does it mean to be a victim of injustice, and why? What does it mean to be a Jew? And the condition of the stranger appeared to me then as truly being the condition of practically all of the world.

Things have become such that no one is any longer able to be satisfied by any answer.

LIBÉRATION: One finds this feeling of strangeness in all of your books. Isn't it actually tied to that experience of the desert of which you've spoken? But at the same time isn't it the experience of writing itself?

E. JABÈS: That's correct, the ground of these books is the desert, that infinity where there is nothing. It's fundamentally the white page. My questioning, my obsession with the book, may very well have been born from that white page, which becomes written. I never thought of a Mallarméan book, of a totality. To think of a book in advance, as a project, is to limit it. The book for me should be without limits, like the desert, thus an exploded book.

The form imposed itself of itself, a desert form whose only limits are the four horizons. The persons themselves are engaged in an immense dialogue in the form of aphorisms, in time and outside of time. They are the voices which explode the book and the place.

Now, that place is also the obsession with god. In the Jewish tradition one of the names of god is PLACE. God is the insupportable absence of the desert. For me, this isn't the god of religions. I've often been called a mystic because I use the word *god*. But it's a word in the dictionary. If you don't use it in literature it's because you fear it, so that you give it precisely the meaning you'd give it believing in it. For me, it's the word of absence, a kind of unthought, an unthinkable something which forces the questioning even farther. God is also the word itself, every word torn apart by what is boundless.

If one reduces the word to what it signifies, one suffocates it. You have to allow it the possibility of opening itself up to all the words that inhabit it. And yet, despite the illimitable aspect of language, I hold very much to the precision of words and sentences. There is no point in breaking up vocables. One must not force the opening. It's the other, the reader, who's going to open the words and the meanings. Precision is a door. What the reader's going to find behind it depends very much on himself.

That's what my struggle with writing's about: moving from the greatest precision in order to get to the largest opening. And what I tell you of words, I could also say of each book which contains in itself other books, which opens out to other books.

LIBÉRATION: And yet, despite these openings, these explosions, one perceives an evident unity throughout your books.

E. JABÈS: I believe the unity comes first of all from the insistence on questioning which never exhausts itself, is rediscovered from one book to the next but after passing through a kind of forgetting of itself. For example, in the first book one meets a questioning which moves toward a first answer. It turns out unsatisfying. In the third book one returns to the same question with a different answer. It is the unpredictable development of the same questioning which creates the unity and at the same time provokes different readings each time, forcing a reperceiving of the preceeding books. Thus the reading is continually without support.

LIBÉRATION: You place great confidence in the reader?

E. JABÈS: Of course. The role of the reader is essential. Because of his having no real foundation, he is constantly pushed beyond himself into his own questioning. Reading the second book, he finds himself asking if he's read the first clearly. Reading the third, he finds himself perceiving that what he thought most important in his reading to that point has perhaps totally vanished, that there is something more important which he'd not seen before. It's an endlesss reading because one's continually returning to the point of departure.

LIBÉRATION: And yet there's a constant progression in each book and from one book to the next; does the point of departure move?

E. JABÈS: It moves because in reality there is no point of departure. That's what I wanted to get to. There is no origin. You've heard it said a lot that these books develop a theory. I don't think one can say that. At every turn I've tried by means proper to the writings to make things be seen physically without theoretical explanations. And one of the means is the questions and answers of the characters. These characters are always in the past. Their words are followed by "he said," "she declared." But now, in the present, what exists? Nothing. There's the beginning. It isn't a question of a nostalgic return to the past. The past is what opens to the ever unknown present.

LIBÉRATION: But it's also the present of the reading, that reading which escapes you, Edmond Jabès, with all the possible readings of your books that you cannot foresee.

E. JABÈS: I've always said that there should be no privilege given for an author's reading. It's one reading among others. To write is to make a particular reading of the book. Moreover I've been able to observe that there have been all kinds of different readings of these books. I am not a believer nor am I religious and yet there have been readings by very believing, very religious readers, which have overwhelmed me. Furthermore, at the outset, one didn't know exactly how to grasp these books. The editor himself didn't know under what heading he should announce them. Opening implies that one accepts the consequences, every possible reading, even those most remote from one's own.

LIBÉRATION: Aren't these inexhaustible readings of the same book precisely the Jewish tradition you're recapturing?

E. JABÈS: Yes, in several ways. My books are for me both a place of passage and the only place where I might live. Isn't it surprising that the word of God should come from the desert, that one of the names of God in Hebrew should be PLACE, and that the book should have been lived as the place of the word by the Jews for millennia? But at the same time I don't accept the book as it is. I believe that the refusal is what one also finds in the Jewish tradition.

The Hebrew people obliged Moses to break the tablets. The origin of the Book therefore comes to pass by a breakage. It's as if the Hebrews had set Moses aside in order to enter into a direct relationship with the Book, without an intermediary, in order to make the text equivalent to God. That invisible God whose name itself is unpronounceable.

There only remains the text, the word. The Jews never stop questioning the Book because their truth is there. And at the same time it's there that they can practice their liberty, that liberty which was refused them everywhere else. One finds that same demand for interpretation, inscribed in Semitic languages, where there are no vowels. Very different words are written in the same way, with the same consonants. So it's always a language to decipher, where everything is not given.

LIBÉRATION: But what does this book, which you are writing in a series of volumes, finally mean to you?

E. JABÈS: That's difficult to say. For me at bottom it was literature, a book destined for writers, for poets. But at the same time I didn't know exactly what it was. I was discovering the book as I wrote it: in some way as a perpetual beginning through writing. Each word has its own life and my life participates in that life of words. When one says that the book rejects us, he's wrong. It simply demands that we let it speak for itself.

It's as if at some moment the book said to me: "Now that, for me, you've said the essential, I can finally express myself. If you intervene, if you add your voice, you'll falsify everything."

Writing has its own movement. It needs to let things ripen, to digest things before it can reveal them. Then the intervention of the writer becomes a superfluous intervention. That's one of the reasons why the traditional novel has always irritated me.

The novelist is most often someone who doesn't listen to the book but wants only to make himself heard. He imposes his characters, his story. And the writing does nothing but repeat. So it becomes a tool, a simple instrument of communication. But writing is entirely another thing.

What's also curious is that one very quickly perceives that one never expressed himself better than when he is silent and lets the writing speak for itself. Each time one wants to force it, one betrays it. I don't mean that there's no need to correct a text. In my case, every book has had no less than three or four versions. But that work is one of *listening*.

LIBÉRATION: Since we're now at the center of the question of writing, I'd like to return to what you said earlier. You've spoken of voices. Sarah, Yukel, Yaël, Elya, Aely are voices, characters who speak. And then there are the voices of the rabbis, which are different. It seems to me that in your books the word plays an essential role. And at the same time you say that the writer's word should efface itself before the writing.

E. JABÈS: Your question seems to me to be important. To mark what is the word of the book and not my (word), I use the word "vocable." This word has for a long time been completely rejected by writers. I use a dictionary a good deal and when I see "archaic" it pains me. There is the Greek *logos*, the Latin *vocabulum*. In French, we should rediscover the word "vocable." The French *parole*, ("word") comes from the Church, from the parable of Christ. Vocable for me is close to being a neologism, it's the word of the book.

LIBÉRATION: In introducing this notion of the word of the book, you completely transgress the classical dichotomy in our culture between speech and writing.

E. JABÈS: Yes. That perhaps comes from the fact that I've lived in the East where spoken stories enjoy a great prestige. In fact I believe I'm a visual man; it's necessary for me to see the words. And at the same time I am very sensitive to hearing them.

There's also the musical aspect of the sentence. Assonance is in a certain sense repetition but it is also an undermining within the repetition. Which makes for a danger. Because the music of the sentence flatters the ear. But there is a better way of hearing everything that is despoiled and destroyed at the same time in writing. Which passes through the white spaces that become for me a part of writing.

Many young writers imagine that the white space gives value to the text. But the whiteness is much stronger, more violent than the text. So it overwhelms the other. It's necessary that writing have a great space in and of itself to support the white spaces.

LIBÉRATION: The white space is also the end. What is the end of the book, of a book, for you? It seems to me that from the beginning, from the first *Book of Questions*, the end has always been present in your books as a point of reference.

E. JABÈS: In fact, in the last three volumes, *The Book of Resemblances*, one always finds a questioning of the same book, but this time through the bias of resemblance. We're all victims of resemblances. We are labeled, we are attributed to something else. And the reader goes more easily for something that resembles something he already knows. Each of these books ends in a trial. The first trial is where the judges do not understand that a writer might say that the book doesn't exist, that a Jew might say that Judaism doesn't exist, that it's an invention. So they accuse him of treason and condemn him. In reality the judge and the accused are both dead. They are spirits. The accused answers: "In order to condemn me, you have had to recognize me, but when I am executed I will truly be a stranger, what I've wanted to be, the stranger from a strange land." In the second book, it's the trial of the judges. They question each other on the criteria for the condemnation they've enacted and end up not knowing whether they themselves are judges, Jews, writers. So they decide no longer to judge. Finally, in the third and last book of that *Resemblances* series, the others condemn the judges. Because if there are no longer any judges, they can no longer know where they stand, what is true and what is not. What does that mean? Maybe nothing. Only that we are full of contradictions, that there is no definitive answer, no truth.

LIBÉRATION: No truth? And yet you've spoken of subversion in your books, or of revolt by the Jews against injustice. So for you, as a writer living in his writing, inhabiting it, what does it mean to say there's no truth? On the plane of social reality? On the plane of politics, ideology?

E. JABÈS: I don't any longer believe that there is any (single) truth there. On the political plane, the answer is always very dangerous. The totalitarian regimes, which live the answer, which impose the answer, cannot tolerate the question. It's necessary to denounce that, and one can only do that by allowing the question, by a critical attitude.

But I believe that many people realize this, these days. We have been so disappointed by everything we've tried to defend that we are obliged to rethink the struggle, to make it less blind. When I was young, I militated a good deal. It was easy then.

On the one hand, you had what was called fascism and on the other what was called democracy. I was eleven years old in 1923 when Mussolini came to power. It was therefore very clear to me: it was necessary to crush fascism. But today it's not always clear what is fascist and what is not.

So even if one believes in a cause, if one sides with a party, it is always necessary to protect the possibility of criticizing—even in a way that's very violent sometimes. We find ourselves confronting a totally open situation that it behooves us to preserve. It's necessary I believe to get used to living with this idea. It is for me, in any event, the only possible certainty, the only one an intellectual can have.

That doesn't mean that at certain moments one shouldn't act within a party, or a group, for a well defined, specific mission that demands attention. But to unconditionally adhere to a "truth" is to renounce one's responsibility as an intellectual. True subversion today is questioning. It also turns up in the Jewish tradition. For example, in this story, which I find very beautiful. A rabbi tells a student: that the commentary of rabbi so-and-so is in my opinion the best that could have been made, that rabbi being the wisest and holiest. Unless there exists another rabbi, whom I don't know, equally wise and equally saintly, who's said the *opposite*. This really corresponds precisely to what I experience today.

We are able to commit ourselves only if we start from what we know, which means always in a limited way. One avoids thereby that rendering experienced by those who've staked everything on a party and suddenly feel themselves betrayed. You can't bet on history, once and for all. Perhaps it's that we're not made for thinking about tomorrow. Every day can put everything back into question. We aren't able to define ourselves in long-range terms.

Besides, what is identity? It's something that's developed every day. If I ask you: who are you, what are you going to say? That you're called so-and-so, that you're the son of so-and-so. But that's not an origin. There is no origin, no identity given once and for all. It's necessary to understand that we only commit ourselves to what we hope to discover.

We have seen intellectuals for example who, after having left the Communist Party, have felt the need to display the reasons for their decision in all the newspapers: as if that departure were dramatic. But it is normal. You've militated for ten years for whatever party and you leave it. And so? You could have lived for ten years in a country and left it. That's what life's about. What I think attracts young people to my books is the large place that has been given to questioning and that has led me to learn to live with my contradictions and the contradictions of others.

The *question* nevertheless allows us to remain vigilant, to assume responsibility for our actions fully. How necessary this vigilance is every instant today! The *question* remains our greatest trump card.

LIBÉRATION: One last question, to extend what you've said earlier: the last book you published last winter—what could you say about it after all you've evoked here?

E. JABÈS: It's first of all a book that should be longer. I've torn up many pages. At bottom, it's a book meant for some close friends. And I've been bowled over realizing that even those friends it was meant for didn't understand it completely. They received it like my other books. At that point I truly felt that one couldn't ever get across all that one means. The last pages of that book are a sort of testament for me. One can't change the way someone reads, even a close friend. That's what the risk of writing is all about too.

Interview by Philippe Boyer, Oct. 18-19, 1980, in *Libération*.
Translation by Jack Hirschman.

Useful Man

You can't work any more. You dream,
    Eyes open, hands open
    In the wilderness
    In the wilderness that plays
With the animals—the useless ones

After the order, after the disorder
In the flat fields, the empty forest
    In the sea heavy and clear
An animal goes by—and your dream
    Is really stillness dreaming

Translation by David Guss from *Les Animaux et Leurs Hommes, Les Hommes et Leurs Animaux*

The Oral &
the Written:
"There is No Written Torah Here on Earth"

THE ORAL TRADITION and the written word complement one another, neither is conceivable without the other. From the outset these two conceptions played a significant part in the thinking of the Kabbalists, who connected them with the mystical symbolism of the *sefiroth* [the ten emanations of God]. The written Torah was looked upon chiefly as a symbol of the giving sphere of the Godhead, identified primarily with the *sefirah Tif'ereth*, while the oral Torah was seen as a symbol of the receptive sphere, which is at once that of the *Shekhinah* and of the "Congregation of Israel." In their active association, these two *sefiroth* manifest the action of God, and similarly the whole revelation of the Torah is given only in this unity of the written and the oral Torah. The forms in which the written and the oral Torah are given here on earth—e.g., the scroll of the Torah and the collections of Talmudic traditions—point back to those deeper spheres from which essentially they arose.…In *Tikkune Zohar*, the author identifies the heart of the organism with the written Torah, the mouth with the oral Torah.

Speculations concerning these two aspects of the Torah are contained in the earliest books of the Kabbalists, the *Book Bahir*, for example. But the most interesting discussion of the relationship between them occurs in a fragment which may be attributable to one of the very first Provençal Kabbalists, namely Isaac the Blind. This fragment, which has come down to us only in manuscript, provides a mystical commentary on the beginning of the *Midrash Konen*, dealing with cosmogony. This midrash repeats the…conception that the pre-existent Torah was written in black fire on white fire, which…Nahmanides already took as an indication of the mystical status of the Torah.

Here the Torah seems to burn before God in black fiery letters on white fire, and it is this conception which inspired Rabbi Isaac, probably before Nahmanides, to write the following:

> In God's right hand were engraved all the engravings [innermost forms] that were destined some day to rise from potency to act. From the emanation of all [higher] *sefiroth* they were graven, scratched, and molded into the *sefirah* of Grace (*hesed*), which is also called God's right hand, and this was done in an inward, inconceivably subtle way. This formation is called the concentrated, not yet unfolded Torah, and also the Torah of Grace. Along with all the other engravings [principally] two engravings were made in it. The one has the form of the written Torah, the other the form of the oral Torah. The form of the written Torah is that of the colors of white fire, and the form of the oral Torah has colored forms as of black fire. And all these engravings and the not yet unfolded Torah existed potentially, perceptible neither to a spiritual nor to a sensory eye, until the will [of God] inspired the idea of activating them by means of primordial wisdom and hidden knowledge. Thus at the beginning of all acts there was pre-existentially the not yet unfolded truth [*torah kelulah*], which is in God's right hand with all the primordial forms [literally: inscriptions and engravings] that are hidden in it, and this is what the Midrash implies when it says that God took the primordial Torah (*torah kedumah*), which stems from the quarry of "repentance" and the source of original wisdom, and in one spiritual act emanated the not yet unfolded Torah in order to give permanence to the foundations of all the worlds.

The author goes on to relate how from the not yet unfolded Torah, which corresponds to the *sefirah* of Grace, there sprang the written Torah, which corresponds to the *sefirah* of Divine Compassion, which is *tif'ereth*, and the oral Torah, corresponding to the power of divine judgment in *malkhuth*, the last *sefirah*. He interprets the fiery organism of the Torah, which burned before God in black fire on white fire, as follows: the white fire is the written Torah, in which the form of the letters is not yet explicit, for the form of the consonants and vowel points was first conferred by the power of the black fire, which is the oral Torah. This black fire is like the ink on the parchment.

"And so the written Torah, can take on corporeal form only through the power of the oral Torah, that is to say: without the oral Torah, it cannot be truly understood." Essentially only Moses, master of all the Prophets, penetrated in unbroken contemplation to that mystical written Torah, which in reality is still hidden in the invisible form of white light. Even the other Prophets gained only a fleeting glimpse of it in momentary intuitions.

The mystical symbolism of this profoundly meaningful passage conceals the view that, strictly speaking, there is no written Torah here on earth. A far-reaching idea! What we call the written Torah has itself passed through the medium of the oral Torah, it is no longer a form concealed in white light; rather, it has emerged from the black light, which determines and limits and so denotes the attribute of divine severity and judgment. Everything that we perceive in the fixed forms of the Torah, written in ink on parchment, consists, in the last analysis, of interpretations of definitions of what is hidden. *There is only an oral Torah*: that is the esoteric meaning of these words, and the written Torah is a purely mystical concept. It is embodied in a sphere that is accessible to prophets alone. It was, to be sure, revealed to Moses, but what he gave to the world as the written Torah has acquired its present form by passing through the medium of the oral Torah. The mystical white of the letters on the parchment is the written Torah, but not the black of the letters inscribed in ink. In the mystical organism of the Torah the two spheres overlap, and there is no written Torah, free from the oral element, that can be known or conceived of by creatures who are not prophets.

Excerpted from *On the Kabbalah and Its Symbolism*. Translated from the German by Ralph Manheim.

Deep Throat: The Grail of the Voice

SOME PROPOSITIONS, first, about our overall subject, the searching for alternatives to the aesthetics of the text; and then some remarks about recent theater history, out of personal memory and actual theaterwork, reflecting on the propositions, or subtextually glancing off:

In over thirty years in the theater, I've lived through the distinction between the literature and the performance and have also been involved in performance which seems to have discarded the literature. But I want to start by saying that, whatever the aesthetics, there is *no* alternative to the text. I think that's so in the final analysis of "the final finding of the ear" (Stevens), the *sounding* of a text down to the last fugitive syllable, or phoneme, when the words seem to have left the page as if there had never been any words, dematerialized in the air. I think that's so even when you think you're sounding without words, only to discover that you're *being-sounded*, verbatim, as if the words being denied are the words being performed, reading you out as on a computer, word for word, spectral as they are, the metaphysical "temptations, indraughts of air" around thought, as Artaud perceived in his onomatopoeic madness.

There is only, so far as memory can reach—through imaginary worlds, perceptual worlds (the world on the screen of the Balinese shadow play described by Stephen Lansing), or the real world (the world on the corporeal screen of the play-within-the-play)—thought echoing thought, sonorously, within the infrastructure of thought, even in silence, like the revolution against reason, which can only be made within it, even in madness...word within word unable to speak a word, *more or less*, more or less theologically, phallologocentrically (the radical feminists say), even when the Word—like Artaud's "dispersion of timbres," the sonorous incantations—seems secularized, shredded, musicated, scattered, or otherwise abolished or vanished.

That was the lesson not only of Derrida's critique of Foucault on *Madness and Civilization* but also of the last generation of theater practice. In the theater we've been through a period where, if the beginning wasn't the Word—the authorizing text—the body became the book and "the grain of the voice" a grail. The phrase is Roland Barthes' in his concept of *writing aloud*, like a desideratum of theater, deep-throated, diapasoned, tongued, "the patina of consonants, the voluptuousness of vowels, a whole carnal stereophony:...the breath, the gutturals, the fleshiness of the lips, a whole presence of the human muzzle...throwing, so to speak, the anonymous body of the actor into [the] ear: it granulates, it crackles, it caresses, it grates, it cuts, it comes: that is bliss." Or, untranslatably, *jouissance*. Or so it seemed.

It wasn't until the first period, however, when language was exhorted to wrap itself carnally around its own phonic substance, the brute materiality of no-presence but its own self-composing force, erotic, somatic and subliminal, ecstatic and even sublime. As Hugo Ball wrote about the polyphonic performance of Dada: "The subject of the *poème simultané* is the value of the human voice. The vocal organ represents the individual soul, as it wanders, flanked by supernatural companions. The noises represent the inarticulate, inexorable and ultimately decisive forces which constitute the background. The poem carries the message that mankind is swallowed up in a mechanistic process. In a generalized and compressed form, it represents the battle of the human voice against a world which menaces, ensnares and finally destroys it, a world whose rhythm and whose din are inescapable."

That was another country and a pre-cybernetic world. The wandering soul is a romantic legacy mourning, through the clamorous Dada manifestations, the absence of a spiritual world, toward the remembrance of which Ball eventually withdrew in relative monastic silence. One of his supernatural companions, Tristan Tzara, had foreseen some inevitable fusion of ecstacy and high tech—"the trajectory of a word, a cry thrown into the air like an acoustic disc"—but even he might have been astonished when it was picked up by a satellite and transmitted everywhere, raising the decibel level. And as the silicon chips take over, we worry as the voice rises that we are merely becoming a part of the *noise*—that the rhythm is so inescapable, the means of distribution so insidious, that the battle can hardly be waged.

As for alternatives to the text, in this serial, cyclical, and solipsistic time, it also seems—when all that was formerly said is done, *voiced*, in ideographs of self-reflexive sound—that we move off the page to realize (again) that, at least for us, the oral tradition is *written* and the performer's body inscribed. Anybody who has been around actors' improvisations will know what I mean. The aleatoric spontaneity is a repertoire of cliché, in the body, in the voice, in the whole carnal stereophony, until—the defences exhausted over long duration—there arises, sometimes, a *structure of apprehension* which really fleshes out a thought.

Which is to say, perhaps, what some spiritual disciplines appear to say, or Shakespeare's *Sonnets*—an authoritative text on sounding and *jouissance* (the prophetic *voice* of the wide world dreaming on things to come)—that however it granulates or crackles, when the *jouissance* comes it comes, like love, in the Idea of loving, however much in the body, very much in the mind. And the phenomenology of the voice still seems in complicity with a metaphysics that teases out a thought. Which is why Shakespeare could have the longing lover of the sonnets, who thinks he is not *thought of* and wants desperately to be with the other *totally, totalled* in thought: "But ah, thought kills me that I am not thought…" As I've said elsewhere, theoretically, that may be the most compulsive passion of theater.

Lest we lose ourselves in that thought, let me return to actual theater practice. I'd like to look back briefly over the last generation when there was much experiment in "the oral mode," attached to the notion of body language, Love's Body, as they used to say, with more or less polymorphous perversion.

In the beginning there was Lee Strasberg who, as you may have heard, died the other day (the same day as another ideologue of sound, Thelonious Monk). The sound sponsored by Strasberg at the Actors Studio, in the self-reflexiveness of the Method, was the voice of the autonomous self: psychological, provincial, "truthful" to the origins of the self, thus not a borrowed voice; to be truthful, ethnic, and at its most self-indulgent (at a loss for origins?) if not pathological, narcissistic.

The Method was an extrapolation from Stanislavski's concepts of sense and emotional memory and Public Solitude to the self-saturation of the Private Moment. The extremity of the Private Moment for the Method actor (of whom Marlon Brando is the archetype) is—for maximum truth of emotion, insensibly there—the moment of an almost unspeakable, maybe illicit incitation, at the brink of transgression or taboo, like a rape that has never been confessed or breaking the incest barrier or some actual or desired self-mutilation—what in the repertoire of postmodern sexuality is being played out in S&M or B&D. In the Performance Art of the gallery scene, we see a conceptualized equivalent of the Private Moment in, say, the autoperformances of Vito Acconci, such as *Seedbed*, where he masturbates soundingly through an amplifier while hidden under a ramp, or decorates his penis mutely in a closet. The theater inevitably raises questions, however, because of its obsession with exposure and the memory of itself as a public form, as to how much privacy in performance can be entertained.

There were, I should say in all fairness, considerable virtues in the Method that we are now beginning to appreciate again. In the return from a non-verbal theater of role transformations or unmediated reflections of the self to plays of character and dialogue, we realize that the actors from the Studio were better equipped for developing character than those who were doing sound/movement exercises in La Mama through plotless "tasks," activities, and games. If there was too much sympathetic affection and false empathy in the Studio, there was also a technique for crossing the distance to character, *becoming the other*, a greater specificity of social behavior, more attentiveness to time and place. But time and place could be, as I've suggested, very local, ingrown, with a deficient sense of history; and the vices of the Method led in the fifties to a tedious psychologizing corresponding to the emergence of packaged therapies, and a reification of very limited forms of personal or confessional experience. "Attention must be paid," they said in *Death of a Salesman*, one of the better plays in that tradition. But when we tried to pay attention, sometimes we couldn't hear.

I mean at rehearsal *and* performance: *Speak up! we can't hear you!* was the director's refrain. I can't tell you how many times I said that to actors during that period, or how many times, wanting to say it, I kept it under my breath. For we are talking about an ethos and, implicitly, a critique of the theater's responsibility, no longer taken for granted, to "communicate" with an audience. There were, as the director bit his tongue, all the conceptual, ethical, and aesthetic intricacies of whether the actor *should* be heard, at what distance?, overheard or—at the margins of perception—not heard at all. It was a considerable crisis in a theater still predicated on a psychology of realism, like the arguments over whether or not, at any distance, an actor should wear makeup. It was also a question of "authenticity."

To pass in and out of hearing was an equivocal response to what was then called the Identity Crisis. What was not heard would be—so far as the dramatist's words were concerned—more or less "line perfect," but it was on the way, refusing to be heard, to a more conscious rejection of the text. The actor who was self-determining by refusing more voice may have learned later, encouraged by Brecht on ideological grounds, not only to withhold the voice but, if he couldn't agree with the text, to rewrite it—or to discard it altogether. To some of us, that seemed a necessary conceptual advance.

There was, however, the worst of it, having nothing much to do with principle or the Alienation-effect, for which purpose Brecht also wanted the actor to speak up. I mean by the worst of it what became for a while the scratch-and-mumble T-shirt school of acting on television, in the image of Brando, who created the image in principle but who, in *Apocalypse Now*, was a parodied whisper of himself. Politically—in the period of what *TIME* named the Silent Generation—it seemed that the whispers and mumbles were the objective correlative of a kind of deliquency, the refusal to speak up so as to be "committed," the quietism of the Cold War and the Age of Ike. When we came to the new conservatism of Ronald Reagan, there was talk of a return to the fifties, which might be so were it not for the shift from an economy of abundance to an economy of scarcity and the inequities of Reaganomics. The non-commitment of that other period may have been, though, an early adumbration of a new deliquency, as if, having run of things to *say*, we say them over and over through the non-semantic poetry of the deconstructed word, tape-looped and tautological, or the repetitive sonorities of Philip Glass—the trickle-down solipsism of a libidinal economy, with supply-side electronics.

But to stay with that other period and fill in the history:

In the fifties and the early sixties there was a lot of justifiable complaint about the vocal incapacities of American actors. The truth is that very few of them had any sort of extensive vocal training, whatever the method—or any concept of the voice, no less its metaphysical dependence on the enigma of a theological presence, what Derrida writes about in "*La parole soufflée*," one of his essays on Artaud, who felt that from the moment of birth his voice, his birthright, was stolen away.

It was a time, too, when we knew very little about *the vocal image* or theater as a structure of phonic or graphic signs; nor did we think so subtly of speech, as Artaud did, "as an active force [like the coiled sleeping serpent of Quetzalcoatl] springing out of the destruction of appearances in order to reach the mind itself" instead of representing itself "as a completed stage of thought which is lost at the moment of its own exteriorization." Derrida writes of the consciousness which enfevered Artaud; that something is being dictated so that the signifier says something more than I mean to say, that metonymic disaster of speech in which, it seems, "the cyclonic breath [*souffle*] of a prompter [*souf-fleur*] who draws his breath in...robs me of that which he first allowed to approach me and which I believed I could say *in my own name*." If there is an ontological theft in the background of performance, it is "a total and original loss of existence itself," thought flying up, the body remaining below, bereaved by the duplicity of escaping words, which are not our own to begin with.

The real depth of the onlogogical cause wasn't what disturbed us in the sixties, the subtle subversion of signification. The actors weren't conscious of it, even when they became aware of Artaud. If the body was bereft, it wasn't because of *la parole soufflée*, but rather, simply, because the throat so often hurt, through plain misuse or abuse. Actors had poor voices and didn't know how to take care of them—to breathe, to use the diaphragm, resonate, project, cadence the complex rhetoric of a classical speech, even if they had the stamina for it, no less think of themselves as the possible instruments of a sound poetry fusing the ideographic body with the revolutionary semiotics of the tape machine, which could disperse semantic meaning into an alphabet of signs and, presumably, divest performance of the surreptitious corruption of the phallocentric presence in the hegemony of the Word.

It was another sort of presence that distressed the actors in San Francisco in the early sixties. When we first introduced electronic music at The Actor's Workshop—I was collaborating then with Morton Subotnick, when he was just starting the Tape Music Center—the actors were intimidated by the potential magnitudes of processed sounds. How can we match that? they thought. Subotnick did a score for our production of *King Lear* which was an experimental model of feasible integration, the actors' voices embedded in the sound, rising over it, laminated, voice embracing sound, extended, random and concrete sounds suspended in the risible air, stage-struck, like visible signs, performing, the storm itself appearing (through multiple speakers strategically deployed) as a dimensionless sonic space, immense, the actual stage expanded, as if the music were in all its inexhaustible and exhausting amplitude the very breathing thought of Lear. (I have written about this production, and the conception behind the score, in *The Impossible Theater: A Manifesto* [New York: Macmillan, 1964, pp. 277-92].) Our actors at The Workshop eventually learned, as they said, once the risk was applauded, to sing along with Subotnick, or other composers, but the work we did with electronic sound was, in the overall scene of American theater, a very isolated experiment.

There still isn't much of it on that scale, or with anything like that complexity. I remember, too, when we went to New York the actors at Lincoln Center, many of whom had come out of the Studio with Elia Kazan, thinking I was out of my mind when they first heard sound textures from the score Subotnick was composing for our first production there; and then the sound and fury about the music, by critics and others, when we actually used it in performance. But back in San Francisco, despite these experiements, we were still very concerned—and for good reason, it was true all over the coun-try—about the sound-producing capacities of the actor in an unaccomodated and unamplified body.

At the end of the sixties, as the Regional Theaters which had struggled for survival were more or less securely established, there was a concerted attack on the problem of the voice, along with greater attention to training for the actor, sponsored by the Ford Foundation. It was obviously with the intention of preparing inadequate American actors to be adequately British, but with some meditated accent, in clasical plays. If we were wary of the British model so far as it was merely rhetorical, with a questionable "inner life" (the Angries were to change that by borrowing a realistic guttiness from Ameri-ca), we nevertheless found a saviour from England, a young woman named Kristin Linklater, who was surprised if delighted to find herself in that role—since she had no extensive credentials either but had been, as I recall, a stu-dent of the woman who had taught Olivier and the Old Vic.

Kristin Linklater's work was patient and effective so far as it went, but it went on the whole very slowly, proceeding from the smallest sound. There was excellent attention to centering, breathing, and relaxation of the body, but the relaxed body tautened again under stress of performance, and there was something in the process that parsed out the voice as something of an enigma. If we saw improvement there was also—not only with the Linklater method, but with others as well—further mystification. The more voice work we did, the more mysterious, it seemed, the voice became. And there was often so much self-consciousness about the voice, such protectiveness, that as soon as anything went wrong in the psychology of the actor, it was if there had been no training, the throat clutched, and the voice went out first of all. Indeed, so long as behavioral psychology remains, even in classics, in the center of the stage, with the obligation to perform something other than a dispossessed or unmediated self (and even then), the voice remains a prob-lem—no matter how strong it otherwise is.

Meanwhile, however, the decibel count was also rising with the political activism of the sixties. The stridency in the streets was matched by the primal screams in the workshops. It was not quite the scream of the Chinese actor outvoicing the desert wind and thereby acquiring, as Artaud imagined, some primordial power in the contest; but there was a very elemental work done with the voice as the actors learned to engage their bodies, taking greater risks. That work expanded the repertoire of performance possiblities through psycho-physical exercises, some invented, some borrowed from other cultures, not only from the Chinese actor, but the Indian, Balinese, Japanese, and from the spiritual disciplines like Yoga. There was also the impact of Jerzy Grotowski who, seizing upon Artaud's vision of the actor signalling through the flames, advanced the concept of the holy actor, shamanistic, burning the body away and leaving visible impulses or holographic signs resonating, a *via negativa* in which the high frequency of metaphysical being is like a Tantric power diagram, where every color of the emotions is the inciting register of a concurrent sound.

It was in this atmosphere that my own work on the voice developed as a further articulation of the methodology of the KRAKEN group. That work was an intense activity of mind, highly verbal, physically charged, like a kind of brain fever in the body, caught up almost acrobatically in the incessant ghosting of thought. I had over the years become familiar with almost all of the available systems of vocal training for the actor, and had worked with some of the better-known teachers. I admired aspects of these other systems but remembered from long experience in various kinds of theater the distress signals of voice in the discomfited actor who might show much improvement in the training but would regress through rehearsal and performance, despite the exercises and the warmups. The methods also seemed to me at times needlessly slow and usually better when actors were being instructed individually, one on one, though we wanted a collective method. I wanted a way, moreover, to exercise the voice that would be at every moment inseparable from the art of acting, something of a performance itself.

What evolved can't really be separated from the investigative procedures of the group, the reflective disposition of all its exercises, of which I used to say that they are all, the innumerable variations, only *one*. The Vocal Sequence we developed was the result of considerable trial and error and also draws upon vocal ideas and exercises familiar in other forms of training. But the distinguishing feature of the work is that every exercise *is* an idea, a heuristic concept. It is not so much the particular element of the sequence which is distinctive, but rather the *sequencing* itself, the structural dynamic of its conception, the momentum of execution, the *idea* of a performance, and the particularity with which the particulars are rehearsed, moving into a performance through what we called *the teleology of an impulse.* By this we mean—even in silence or seeming stasis—the following through of any gesture, physical or vocal, at any behavioral level, recognizably mimetic or utterly abstract, as if it were ordained, *inscaped,* moving once committed toward the consummation, *beyond exhaustion,* of something generic, some indeterminate and (sub)liminal choice.

There is not, so far as I know, any vocal idea, any conceivable way of using the voice which is not suggested by the Vocal Sequence that follows below. The emphasis is on vocal *production* but with attention to articulations and within the structuring of *perception.* There is a perceptual issue posed by every increment of the sequence or, as that occurs, the interchangeability of elements, the transposition being the act of perception as well. So, when at the beginning of the sequence, there is a movement from silence to audibility, the perceptual question involved has to do with the threshold moment when audibility is *achieved,* for whom? at what distance? self-reflexively or projected? and even before that, the precise determination of the threshold moment when sound *materializes* on the lips or, with a view to the reflexive moment of the origin of the sound, the decisive moment when, out of silence, the lips begin to move. Certain moments of the sequence have, if conceived through performance, what Artaud speaks of as a *"metaphysics-in-action"* or ontological implications, like the gathering and reduction of sound in (7), where the sound may go through a diminuendo of being until, like the spotlight of Emmett Kelley, gathered into absence, it disappears.

The Vocal Sequence wouldn't have taken the form it did were it not for a whole series of Impulse Exercises developed along with the vocal work. These were meant to explore marginal and transformative states, exponential limits, in which the actors could make the exploration only by exceeding themselves. The idea of the Impulse Exercises was absorbed into the structure of the Vocal Sequence, as indicated in the version here. That version is what was written down for the actors in KRAKEN after much experiment with the disposition of the initiating elements and the sequencing of the entire structure. We have given demonstrations of the Vocal Sequence, and those who have seen it may remember it as a performance in which the elements are orchestrated with collective and solo variants, permutated, syncopated, single voices rising, antiphonal, as if the prescribed order of elements was the basic melody of the sequence which is disrupted and dispersed by improvisation, as in a jazz ensemble, and *reconstructed* in the playing out—a playing out, however, without closure. We have also performed the Vocal Sequence within other structures of performance, as in the extraordinary ramification of the basic mirroring exercise—known in almost every acting technique—which, in our work, becomes an epistemological field, "mirror upon mirror mirrored...all the show" (Yeats), a *power structure* whose determining source of energy is obscure, once the mirror is in motion, not only to those observing but to those performing it as well—although the formal power *of* the structure is inarguable.

The sequence is taught with the elements in the order indicated, but the actors in KRAKEN have long become accustomed to modulating the sequence as if it were—after the movement from silence to introjection—a combinatory set or a palette of vocal options whose limits are indeterminable. Because our work has been so obsessively concerned with the problematic of language, the sequence is never performed without words. The text of the sequence which follows, let me emphasize, was prepared for the actors and addressed to them. It assumes their familiarity with a number of techniques or exercises named which should not, however, make for any problems in following the principles and design of this approach to the voice. Since we have also taught the Vocal Sequence in workshops, some of the introductory remarks are anticipatorily responding to certain well-known anxieties and arguments over the voice. First of all, that it should be used organically, not artificially; or the ambiguity as to which comes first, body gesture or vocal expression. Grotowski says body first, then voice, but I think that's a non sequitur, as the introduction suggests:

Vocal Sequence

This is designed as a structure for searching with the voice, searching out the possibilities of voice. The body will automatically be involved, organically—that's unavoidable, and the voice can originate nowhere else but in the body, propelled by it and propelling. The rapidity with which it should eventually be done and the rhythmic play of it should eliminate interferences that come from wondering which comes first, voice or body—the emphasis is on the voice as body language.

Take a verse passage or any other speech, and use the voice as the instrument of investigation; not as the outcome of another process as if it were not part of the body. Do the following in a series, repeating any part at will, and after slow motion in any order, though you will eventually want to score it in very personal ways. Remember: the structure allows for "recovering the losses" whenever you feel the voice has overstretched itself; it can always be brought in, introjecting or silently, but also remember that the point is to *stretch* the voice, in amplitude and articulation. There is a kind of dramatic structure involved, with climactic sequences of diminishment and expansion, speed, and the expansion and contraction of space. The climaxes should be attempted, gradually building by some means of returning to a center or altering impulse, but the superobjective is to discover and exercise the range of the voice. Other elements may be added and more stringent particulars (e.g., you may only sweep the floor with fricatives; set your own challenges).

When the elements are understood, then the sequence should be performed as an Impulse Exercise, rapidly, without mental interferences, rhythmically, voice, and body; it should be ideographic finally without your thinking of it, the passage you used to motivate it virtually dissolving into the composition of an impulse. In this sequence it's not the passage which is important but the exercise of your voice, though any single exercise in it may be a valuable technique for studying a text. *You are acting/performing all the time.*

1) *Speak silently*, gradually moving up to the level of audibility; a precise sense of when the words pass over your lips. Start without lip movement.

2) *Speak normally*: point of focus necessary, moving from relatively close to some distance ("stage" distance) you can reach without shouting.

3) *Slow motion*: exploring personal values of each word; exploring images behind the words; exploring the phonemic structure of the words, vowels and consonants; different varieties of slow motion, biting words or caressing with air, exploring words as if they floated in space, etc.

4) *Introjecting*: the opposite of projecting, but also—as in psychological terminology—incorporating the words; speak as if relating outward, but address speech to the inner ear, as in a subjectively played soliloquy. In this and slow motion, the act of reflection is inevitable.

5) *Project atmosphere*: assertion of distinct presence by means of voice; as when a person walks into a room, he brings an atmosphere (what Michael Chekov means in connection with radiation of character); but the voice does it; change atmosphere.

6) *Speak from imaginary center*: moving at will; movement will naturally be incited by previous sequences.

7) *Diminish and expand*: also reverse, like Emmett Kelley's spotlight, or any other image that serves—images will be invoked by all sequences, or will propel sequences.

8) *Line by line ideographs*: speak line, make gesture, let gesture condition next line; also word by word.

9) *Faster and faster*: keep increasing the speed to the limit of intelligibility; slow down, then see if you can take it further. Intelligibility is always the limiting condition at any point in the sequence; you may stretch beyond but should be able to make it clear by exploring the problem of articulation at any limit.

10) *Densities*: harden the air, pack it, soften the air; gravity or weightlessness; the vocal equivalent of the Space Substance exercise in movement.

11) *Expand space, contract space*: this combines imagination with power and concentration; think of the entire space as a resonator, fill it; draw it in by power of will—capacious sound, tight sound, psyche affecting pitch.

12) *Duration*: a critical section in the sequence; an *idée fixe*, obsessionally extended; either a prolonged massing of sound, an almost unnavigable pitch, speed or volume—but a difficult assertion of sound, sustained beyond imagining.

13) *Varying pitch*: low to high and reverse; actually pitch will vary in several of these exercises, although you may want to set as a technical requirement in practicing individual sequences of fixation of pitch. (Relate to *Resonators*: Head, Chest, Laryngeal, Nasal, Occipital, Maxillary, Combinations.)

14) *Perform actions with voice*: cover the wall, drive a nail, put out a match, sweep the floor, tie shoelaces, embrace someone, kiss, assault, kill, etc.

15) *Change character of voice*: voice as axe, scissors, honey (as in Walking Exercise).

16) *Experiment with vowels and consonants, syllable weighting*: this too will occur naturally in previous sections, as in slow motion.

17) *Unusual or Grotesque or Mimetic Sounds*: natural sounds, such as bird, wind, storm, animals—roars, hisses, etc., never-heard sounds.

18) *Mouth sounds*: using lips, hollows, teeth, cheeks, tonguings, spittle; blowing, wheezing, gurgling, razzing, etc.

19) *Laughing/Crying*: this is actually a diaphragmatic exercise as well; keep changing from one to the other, giggles, sobs, hoarse laughter, gasps, etc.

20) *Wailing/Keening*: the wildest lamentations.

Which must be returned to *speech*. Which is to say the production of meaning and semantic continuity. If Wittgenstein cautions us about the limit which defies communication—"What we cannot speak about we must pass over in silence"—Derrida imposes an auditory responsibility: "It remains then, for us to *speak*, to make our voices *resonate* (*resonner*) through the corridors in order to make up for the breakup of presence" (*pour supléer l'éclat de la présence*); which might also mean "in order to supplement the impact of one's presence." That impact is not established merely by the grain of the voice, if the grain of the voice is taken to mean a carnal stereophony without semantic continuity. But that doesn't actually seem to be what Barthes had in mind, as we can see from an essay with that title in which he compares two singers, using Julia Kristeva's distinction between the *pheno-text* and the *geno-text*.

"From the point of view of the pheno-song," which includes everything that pertains to culture, style, communication, expression, representation, the rules of song, "Fischer-Dieskau is assuredly an artist beyond reproach: everything in the (semantic and lyrical) structure is respected and yet nothing seduces, nothing sways us to *jouissance*." It is an art which, respecting the pheno-text, "never exceeds culture: here it is the soul [with its "myth of respiration"—hense *inspiration*] which accompanies the song, not the body." But Panzera, on the contrary, is no mere agency of *pneuma*, the mysticism of the "soul swelling or breaking" with the passion of the lungs. "The lung, a stupid organ (lights for cats!), swells but gets no erection; it is in the throat, place where the phonic metal hardens and is segmented, in the mask that *significance* explodes, bringing not the soul but *jouissance*." What he hears in Panzera is the geno-text, through an extreme rigor of thought which regulates "the prosody of the enunciation and the phonic economy of the French language…"

It is an art totally material *and* totally abstract, and while the space of the voice is an infinite one, its truth hallucinated, that art was achieved in Panzera, according to Barthes' ear, by a patina of consonants, "given the wear of a language that had been living, functioning and working for ages past" and that becomes "a springboard for the admirable vowels." It is *that* patination which fulfills *"the clarity of meaning"*—the grain of the voice in the grain of the language, like the Russian cantor he describes, producing a sound from "deep down in the cavities, the muscles, the membranes, the cartilages, and from deep down in the Slavonic language…the materiality of the body speaking its mother tongue…." What Barthes is objecting to, of course, is known and coded emotion, immunized against pleasure, and reducing meaning to the tyranny of meaning, instead of the writing of the geno-text, which exists in the grain of the language from which the voice draws its sustenance, whatever else the body gives.

Whatever we do with vocal production, it is the grain of the language which eludes us in this country; what made it so hard, for instance, for William Carlos Williams ever to be certain of the variable foot. Barthes worried that with the death of melody, "the French are abandoning their language," if not as normative set of values, then as the site for pleasure, the place "where language works *for nothing*, that is, in perversion…" In our vocal work, we think we have restored that site, that place, although it's hard to abandon a language whose grain has never yet been truly ascertained. That still remains the quest of the voice, the grail, in theater, sound poetry, or on tape.

Herbert Blau's essay was first delivered as a talk at a conference on "Oral Modes in Contemporary Arts and Culture" at the Center for Music Experiment, University of California at San Diego, February 19-21, 1982. The conference also included J. Stephen Lansing's "The Sounding of the Text" (see above).

Contributors

HERBERT BLAU, currently Distinguished Professor of English and Comparative Literature at the University of Wisconsin-Milwaukee, has also had a long career in the theater. His two most recent books are *The Audience* and *To All Appearances: Ideology and Performance.* He is now writing a book on fashion.

EDUARDO CALDERÓN is both a practicing artist and shaman living in the Trujillo area of Northern Peru. He has lectured in Europe and the United States on healing and *curanderismo.*

BECKY COHEN is a free-lance artist/photographer whose areas of activity include fine arts documentation, collaborative work with other artists and writers, and her lifelong devotion to the photographic description of human relationships and to photographing the unclothed human figure. Her photographs have been exhibited in and collected by many museums in both the U.S. and Europe. The photographer is currently living the life of a gypsy; she is looking forward to becoming a wild animal.

PAUL ELUARD (1895-1952) was a writer associated with the Dada and Surrealist Movements in Paris. He published his first book of poetry at the age of eighteen when confined to a Swiss sanatorium for tuberculosis. His books in English translation include *Capital of Pain* and *Selected Poems.*

MICHAEL GIBBS is a British artist, critic and writer living in Amsterdam since 1975. Formerly involved with concrete/sound poetry and artists' publications, he continues to be fascinated by the metaphor of the Book (including its current electronic metamorphosis via the Net).

DAVID GUSS is a poet, translator, editor, folklorist, and anthropologist who has lived and worked in various parts of Latin America. Currently teaching at Tufts University, he is the author of *To Weave and Sing: Art, Symbol, and Narrative in the South American Rain Forest* and *The Festive State: Race, Ethnicity, and Nationalism as Cultural Performance*.

DICK HIGGINS' first regular paid job was rubbing up pre-sensitized photo-offset printing plates after high school. His love of books and of their contents is about equal. Visual artist, poet, composer, performer, scholar and publisher of the legendary Something Else Press, his biography of Merle Armitage is being published in 1997 by David R. Godine.

JACK HIRSCHMAN has written and translated more than seventy-five books and chapbooks of poetry and essays; he translates from eight languages. He has just completed with Boadiba, the Haitian poet, the first major anthology of Creole poetry, *Open Gate*, to be published by Curbstone Press. He lives in San Francisco, where he also paints.

EDMOND JABÈS was born in Cairo in 1912. He left Egypt during the Suez crisis and lived in Paris until his death in 1991. Author of *The Book of Questions, The Book of Resemblances, From the Book to the Book*, among others, Edmond Jabès is widely regarded as one of France's greatest contemporary writers. In 1987 he received France's National Grand Prize for Poetry.

ALISON KNOWLES is a visual artist doing performance, installation and sound art. She makes books and constructs acoustic poems for West German radio. She is known for her Fluxus event scores and the human-scale environments, *The Big Book, The House of Dust* and *The Book of Bean*.

She has taught in California, Salzburg and Hamburg and, in 1996, was Documenta Guest Professor in Kassel, Germany.

J. STEPHEN LANSING holds a joint appointment as Professor of Anthropology in the Department and School of Natural Resources & Environment at the University of Michigan. His fieldwork in Indonesia began in 1971. His most recent books are *Priests and Programmers: Technologies of Power in the Engineered Landscape of Bali* (Princeton University Press, 1991) and *The Balinese* (Harcourt Brace, 1994).

STÉPHANE MALLARMÉ (1842-1898) was a poet whose preoccupation with "the book" opened the door. "Standing in the nineteenth century he set the twentieth in motion." (J.R.)

DAVID MELTZER is a poet, editor, translator and teacher living in California. His most recent book of poetry is *Arrows: Selected Poetry, 1957-1992* (Black Sparrow). He is the editor of *Reading Jazz* and its companion anthology *Writing Jazz*. David Meltzer is on the faculty of the Graduate Poetics Program at New College of California.

TINA OLDKNOW is an art historian specializing in classical antiquity and historical and contemporary glass. She has worked for several museums, including the Los Angeles County Museum of Art; the J. Paul Getty Museum, Malibu; the Henry Art Gallery at the University of Washington, Seattle; and the Seattle Art Museum. Researching apotropaic objects and images—ancient and modern—has been a lifelong interest.

GEORGE QUASHA is the author of several published books of poetry including *Somapoetics*, *Giving the Lily Back Her Hands*, and the forthcoming *In No Time*; has edited several poetry anthologies including *America a Prophecy* and *Open Poetry*; and has been (with Susan Quasha) co-publisher/editor of Station Hill Press in Barrytown, New York since 1978. His ongoing dialogical collaborations with Charles Stein and Gary Hill, begun in the 1970s, include sound and text-related performance, installation art, video art, and "liminal books."

JED RASULA worked as a researcher for the ABC television program "Ripley's Believe it or Not" before taking a Ph.D. in the History of Consciousness at University of California, Santa Cruz. He is the author of a critical history, *The American Poetry Wax Museum: Reality Effects 1940-1990*, and a book of poetry, *Tabula Rasula*. Forthcoming books include *Imagining Language, An Anthology* (co-edited with Steve McCaffery) and *Tactics of Attention*, a collection of essays on poetry and poetics (with Don Byrd). He currently teaches English at Queen's University in Kingston, Ontario.

JEROME ROTHENBERG is the author of over fifty books of poetry including *Poems for the Game of Silence, Poland/1931, A Seneca Journal, Vienna Blood, That Dada Strain, New Selected Poems 1970-1985, Khurbn, The Lorca Variations*, and most recently *Seedings & Other Poems* (all from New Directions). He has also edited six groundbreaking assemblages of traditional and contemporary poetry: *Technicians of the Sacred, Shaking the Pumpkin, America a Prophecy, Revolution of the Word, A Big Jewish Book* [a.k.a. *Exiled in the Word*], and *Symposium of the Whole*. The first volume of a two-volume global anthology of twentieth-century poetry, *Poems for the Millennium: The University of California Book of Modern & Postmodern Poetry* (co-edited with Pierre Joris) was published by the University of California Press in 1995. With his anthologies and journals such as *Alcheringa* and *New Wilderness Letter*, he has long been a central mover in the development of an ethnopoetics "as a necessary component of any truly innovative poetics."

GERSHOM SCHOLEM (1897-1982) is widely regarded as one of the leading authorities on the Kabbalah and Jewish mysticism. His many books include *Major Trends in Jewish Mysticism, On the Kabbalah and Its Symbolism* and *On Jews and Judaism in Crisis*.

DENNIS TEDLOCK is McNulty Professor of English and Research Professor of Anthropology at the State University of New York at Buffalo. His books are *Finding the Center: Narrative Poetry of the Zuni Indians*; *Teachings from the American Earth: Indian Religion and Philosophy* (with Barbara Tedlock); *The Spoken Word and the Work of Interpretation*; *Popol Vuh: The Mayan Book of the Dawn of Life*; *Days from a Dream Almanac*; *Breath on the Mirror: Mythic Voices and Visions of the Living Maya*; and *The Dialogic Emergence of Culture* (with Bruce Mannheim.)

KARL YOUNG tells readers a lot of essentials in "Book Forms," backed up and filled out by his "Notes on *Codex Vienna*." In 1990 he changed the name of his press from Membrane to Light and Dust Books. Work with computer technology and the Internet's World Wide Web now join his other projects.

Colophon

The Book, Spiritual Instrument was set primarily in Scala and Rotis typefaces. It was printed on 70# Fortune Matte paper and smythe sewn at Thomson-Shore in Dexter, Michigan. This first Granary Books edition was published in October, 1996.